THE DESERT IN
THE CITY

THE DESERT IN THE CITY

CARLO CARRETTO

TRANSLATED BY BARBARA WALL

CROSSROAD · NEW YORK

1987
The Crossroad Publishing Company
370 Lexington Avenue, New York, NY 10017

Originally published by Le Edizioni Paoline,
Rome under the title *Il Deserto Nella Citta*.
© Literarisches Institut A G Basel 1978

Copyright in the English Translation
© William Collins Sons & Co Ltd, 1979

Printed in the United States of America

Library of Congress Catalog Number: 81-70877

ISBN: 0-8245-0423-2

CONTENTS

FOREWORD

This book is an attempt to help those people who feel weighed down by work and other commitments, so weighed down that when faced with the demands of prayer they say: I just can't cope with it, I haven't the time, I hardly have time to sleep as it is.

Right. Let's see what we can do about it.
You can find the desert anywhere, even in the city.
It is quite possible once you know how to love.
It is a little more difficult, that's all.
Shall we try?

And remember: the desert does not mean the absence of men, it means the presence of God.

THE REASON FOR
THIS BOOK

Hong Kong, Easter, 1977

I have always been 'surprised' by life.

And as I believe that God is life, just as He is light and love, I have come to the conclusion that it is God Himself who has 'surprised' me on my journey.

God is surprise.

God is novelty.

God is creativity.

After my long period in the Sahara Desert I had the joy of meeting Pope John again. In the course of our interview he looked at me with his lively penetrating eyes and said: 'Tell me, had you ever thought of going to Africa before you actually went there? Was the change in your life premeditated? During your time here in Rome, when you were working for Catholic Action, did you foresee the possibility of becoming a Little Brother? Had you any premonition that your life would change, that you would join a religious order?'

'No,' I said, 'none at all. God's call was a total surprise, as was my decision in the space of a few days to accept what I believed was His will and go off to Africa. Before that moment I had never envisaged a change of direction of that kind.'

Then the Pope looked at me with a smile and said, 'It often happens like that. We end up in places we had never previously dreamed of. It's exactly what has happened to me. It had never entered my mind . . .' And he went on smiling while looking out of the window that gave onto the Lake of Castelgandolfo.

*　　*　　*

And in just such a way God, who is 'surprise', has now brought me to China. The surprise did not lie in my having to make another journey; no, I have made plenty of journeys. The novelty lay in the fact that I did not expect it, and least of all did I expect what He wanted to tell me here in Hong Kong, in this city so like and yet so unlike other cities, and at that vast airport. For at that vast airport men arrive from all the continents of the world, and trade on a world scale is able to make the Chinese from the People's Republic exchange smiles with the Chinese from Formosa; while Japanese, Koreans, Americans, Europeans, Arabs and Indians assemble in the same skyscraper and are all ready to smile if only they can do good business.

Mao Tse Tung said: 'In Hong Kong hens lay golden eggs,' and this was why he maintained it as it was with a special statute even though – had he so wished – he could have occupied it in a few hours.

Hong Kong struck me as being a true city of the future, riding at anchor on limitless waters and with streets improbably scattered with temples dedicated to idols, as were the streets of Corinth and Athens at the time of St Paul. The names of the temples are as follows: The Bank of America, The Hong Kong-Shanghai Banking Corporation, The Bank of China, The Chartered Bank, The Bank of Tokyo, La Banque Nationale de Paris, The Dresner Bank,

The Chase Manhatten Bank, The Hang Seng Bank, The Bank of Bangkok, The Amsterdam Bank, and so on.

It is a pity that these temples all have the same kind of façade and that there is no scope for the imagination in modern idolatry.

But perhaps it is precisely because these temples lack imagination and fantasy that I have been able to find my greatest surprise among the young people of China.

Let me explain.

Knowing about my arrival in Hong Kong, a group of friends had been kind enough to translate my *Letters from the Desert* into Chinese-Cantonese and to get them serialized in the local papers. I don't know how they managed it. All I know is that on my arrival I was besieged by my readers. Nothing of the kind had ever happened to me before. Night and day I was inundated by telephone calls, invitations, requests to address meetings, and so on.

And the theme was always the same: the Gospel of Jesus.

I still see before me the bright eyes of the young Chinese who questioned me passionately on the subject of Christ.

So obviously the temples with their pagan idols had not won over everyone. The spirit of the Lord had breathed on the young workers and intellectuals and students with whom I came into contact and had raised questions in their minds, questions about invisible realities, about the meaning of existence and the purpose of life.

Brother Carlo, tell me how to pray.

Tell me how to think about God's presence in the world.

What does it mean – to create a desert in one's own life?

What does God's 'Kingdom' mean?

How can I live the Beatitudes?

More than anything it was the Gospel that stirred them. These young people, educated in one or other of the various religions of Hong Kong, sensed the oldness of their catechisms, the static quality of their practices, the immobility of their institutions.

It was obvious that they were dissatisfied.

They wanted to hear a new message, and this was to be found in the Gospel of Jesus.

The more they felt that their religion was in crisis, the more the Gospel knocked at their door, and the more actual and enthralling did the breath of the Spirit make it become.

The texts that excited them most were the Beatitudes and those concerning poverty, prayer, commitment, community, equality, non-violence, contemplation, gratuitousness, God's word, the Spirit.

Those young people who had been educated in the great rich schools and colleges of the city felt an attraction towards the poor in the slums, towards the outcasts and the oppressed, and, having abandoned their traditional religious practices, they often gathered together to pray in small spontaneous groups that sprang up more or less anywhere. Where these groups particularly took root was in the innumerable skyscrapers that give Hong Kong first prize for modernity among cities set in a bay, a bay which competes for first prize in beauty with that of Rio de Janiero.

But Hong Kong also competes with Rio for first prize in social distinctions, in the unequal distribution of wealth, in the mixture of the sublime and the horrendous which brings with it the mixture of men who pass by each other with their hidden tears and their thirst for unattainable happiness.

Indeed it is here in Hong Kong, in this city where everyone works like ants, that there is an almost total absence of protection for workers, especially the very poorest. As long as you work and do your bit then you're all right because you are contributing to the creation of the horrible idol of power, but as soon as you're old or ill you're thrown out without a pension or any form of assistance.

A poor and sensitive girl once said to me: 'When my grand-father stopped working he received no help of any kind. He managed to make out for a little while but when he couldn't go on any longer he left a note in the house and threw himself from a rock in the bay. The Chinese often prefer to die quietly by committing suicide rather than be a burden on their large poor family.'

It is appalling!

But it is precisely in these harsh and inhuman conditions that the phenomenon of the Gospel breaks through the earth's crust and surges up into consciousness.

So deeply have I been aware of this that for the first time in my life I have to confess that I have wished to live longer so as to be able to proclaim God's word.

It had never occurred to me to want this before. Whether through weakness, or through knowing well enough what to expect when I die owing to my experience of God, I have always wished not to prolong my sojourn on earth.

I have felt the same as St Paul at the thought of being freed from the weight of the world:

> For me to live is Christ, and to die is gain. If it is to be life in the flesh, that means fruitful labour for me. Yet which I shall choose I cannot tell. I am hard pressed between the two. My desire is to depart and be with Christ, for that is far better. But to remain in the flesh is more necessary on your account. Convinced of this, I know that I shall remain and continue with you all, for your progress and joy in the faith' (*Philippians 1: 21–25*).

It is impossible to express better the inner attitude of someone who lives by faith and feels caught between the love of God which beckons to him and the love of his brothers to which he is committed.

'Yes, I prefer to go but . . . if I can be useful for the sake of the Gospel, then I shall stay.'

In Hong Kong I have felt the joy of living so as to proclaim the Good News.

What happiness to be able to tell people that we are risen in Christ, that history moves towards life not towards chaos, that our tears are counted, that everything has a significance because God is the Living God and the Father.

Yes, it is worth prolonging one's life for this, living for this. It is worth saying with Père de Foucauld:

'For the Gospel I am prepared to go to the ends of the earth and live until Judgement Day.'

★　　★　　★

It was on the seventeenth floor of a huge block of workers' flats that I had arranged to meet some of my young Chinese friends.

We had been talking for hours – about the Gospel, about commitment, about prayer.

Then a student of architecture who lived in Hong Kong (though his parents lived in the People's Republic near Shanghai) suddenly said: 'Brother Carlo, I have been wanting to meet you ever since I read your *Letters from the Desert*. You write so enthusiastically about the time you spent in the Sahara that one gets the impression that there's no substitute for that kind of solitude. But I can't go there. I must find my God here in the Babel of my city. So what do you advise me to do? How should I set about it? Is it possible? And if it is possible, why don't you write a book for us to help us find our desert here in the city?

'And don't forget China.'

I felt deeply moved and at the same time deeply understood.

The young student looked at me with sympathy.

And that was the moment when *The Desert in the City* was born in my heart.

Outside the window it was evening and I saw the great mass of Hong Kong's skyscrapers switching on their lights.

I remembered that I had seen this sight for the first time in New York – skyscrapers with all their lights on. Illuminated skyscrapers look like diamonds.

It seems impossible that such ugly objects should become alive and beautiful when clothed with light.

So there's nothing that is altogether negative. Even the city, sink of iniquity and asphalt jungle, can have its light and its 'transparency'.

'The desert in the city', I repeated over and over to myself, looking out of the window, my thoughts reaching to the distant origin of this word 'desert' which had been laid on my heart at the best moment of my life. I thought back to nights in the Sahara, to the sand-dunes, to all the paths I had trodden, to the search for intimacy with God, to the memorable stars which decorated so discreetly the sweetness of the African nights, deep symbol as they were of the nights in which my faith was immersed and in which I felt so well and so safe.

The real desert, the desert of sand and stars, had been my first love, and I would never have left it had not obedience claimed me from afar.

'Brother Carlo, you have discovered the absolute of God, now you must discover the absolute of man.'

So off I had gone in search of men.

I was thoroughly disorientated and it took me some time to recover my equilibrium and deep joy.

But then God caused me to realize that there was no privileged 'place' where He lived but that everywhere was the 'place' where He lived and that you could find Him anywhere.

'I must create the desert in my own life,' I said to myself as I gradually moved away from the stability of my solitude and walked towards a totally different world.

But this was not enough.

It was necessary for me to experience Hong Kong in order to see that even the city had the potential of the desert and even skyscrapers could become luminous like diamonds.

All you had to do was to turn them around in the darkness of faith until the lights looked like stars.

'I can but try,' I said to my young student. 'I had decided not to write any more books . . . But the theme of "the desert in the city" pleases me. It corrects in me, and in anyone who, like me, is too in love with solitude, the urge to want to flee.'

The temptation is so easy, especially for the violent . . . and the lazy.

Who knows how it'll work out!

God is great!

And then even Sarah's withered womb and Abraham's old age can give birth to a son as beautiful as Isaac . . . if God so wishes.

THE DESERT IN
THE CITY

So here I am, ready to answer all those who have asked for my help in the search for union with God in the city – union with God, intimacy with the Absolute, joy and peace of heart, the presence of the Invisible One, divine reality, the Eternal One. All these, in the city.

It is not going to be easy – let us realize that at once!

We are living in a tragic century in which even the strongest people are tried in their faith.

It is an epoch of idolatry, anguish and fear; an epoch when power and riches have dulled in man's spirit the basic requirement of the first commandment of the Law, 'You shall love God with your whole heart . . .'.

What can we do to dissipate the darkness that oppresses modern man? How can we overcome the noonday devil who attacks the believer in his maturity?

I do not hesitate to give an answer which I myself have put to the test at a difficult moment of my life:

The desert . . . the desert . . . the desert!

I only have to say this word to feel my whole being rise up and move forward even while physically it remains where it is.

It signifies the awareness that it is God who saves, that without

Him I am 'in the shadow of death', and that to emerge from the darkness I must put myself on the path that He Himself will show me.

It is the path of Exodus, it is the march of the people of God from the slavery of idols to the freedom of the Promised Land, to the joy and brightness of the Kingdom.

And this, by crossing the desert.

But the word 'desert' is much more than a geographical expression that suggests to our minds a derelict, parched and arid expanse of land with no-one in it.

The word 'desert' – for the man who lets himself be taken up by the Spirit who animates God's word – expresses the search for God in silence, it is a 'suspension bridge' thrown by the soul in love with God over the dark abyss of its own spirit, over the strange deep crevasses of temptation, over the unfathomable precipices of its own fears which form an obstacle to the progress towards God.

'Yes, such a desert is holy and is a prayer beyond all prayer. It leads to the continuous presence of God and to the heights of contemplation where the soul, at peace at last, lives by the will of Him whom it loves totally, absolutely and endlessly.'[1]

I told you that the word 'desert' means much more than a mere geographical place.

The Russians, who understand these things and are our masters in these matters, call it 'poustinia'.

Poustinia may mean a geographical desert, but at the same time it may mean the place to which the desert fathers withdrew, it may mean hermitage, a quiet place to which people withdraw so as to find God in silence and prayer, a place where – as a Russian mystic living in America puts it – 'we can raise the arms of prayer and

[1] Catherine De Hueck Doherty, *Poustinia*, Cerf, Paris and Fount Paperbacks, London, 1977.

penance towards God in expiation, intercession and reparation for our own sins and the sins of our brothers. The desert is the place where we gather courage, where we pronounce words of truth remembering that God is truth. The desert is the place where we purify ourselves and prepare ourselves to act as if touched by the burning coal that was placed by the angel on the lips of the Prophet.'[2]

The point is – and this is the characteristic that I want to underline – the point is that 'poustinia' for the Russians, as well as for ourselves who are in the same spiritual line of mystical experience, accompanies man wherever he goes and does not abandon him because he is not in the desert.

In other words: if man cannot go to the desert, then the desert can come to man.

That is why we talk about 'making a desert in the city'.

Make yourself a little 'poustinia' in your house, in your garden, in your attic. Do not dissociate the concept of desert from the places where men and women live their lives. Try both in your thoughts and in your lives to put this glorious phrase into practice: 'the desert in the heart of the city.'

Père de Foucauld, one of the most tireless seekers after modern spirituality, set up his hermitage at Béni-Abbès in a context where he could be open to God and at the same time open to men.

And when he decided to build a wall around it he stopped when the wall was two feet high. This was so that the people living in the neighbouring oases could easily climb over it when they wanted to visit him.

The wall remained, however, as a 'sign' of his monastic isolation. The desert occupied his life more profoundly.

Yes, we must create a desert in the heart of crowded places.

It is a practical way of helping people now.

[2] *Ibid.*

It is a pressing problem. It is constantly spoken of.

It is in the air.

Pierre Delfieux, a friend who was with me in the Sahara for two years, has initiated in Paris a form of religious life based on the commitment to live the monastic ideal in that great city – that is to say the ideal of work, prayer, silence, liturgy and love.

I have no hesitation in saying that it will only be a matter of decades before we see the miracle of these foundations in every city, before we see the splendour of men and women transforming 'Babel' into 'Jerusalem' and the 'deportation' into a place of prayer.

★   ★   ★

But for the moment let us start with small things and come back to the initial project. This book was conceived as a help for people who want to spend a week of more intense prayer, and a deeper search for God, in the midst of their daily commitments.

Choose any ordinary week. Don't dream about what might be, but accept reality as it is.

Have a Bible close at hand as your indispensable tool, and concentrate on the love which lies within you.

Don't worry too much about place, because everywhere is God's 'place' and the 'setting' for His presence.

To encourage you let me tell you that at the time of my conversion I made the train the 'place' for my prayer.

My work took me back and forth, and you know what a railway carriage is like when you go to and from the city every morning and evening – cram full of workers and students. Noise, laughter, smoke, bustle, crush.

I sat in a corner and heard nothing.

I read the Gospel.

I closed my eyes.

I spoke and listened to God. What sweetness, what peace, what silence!

The power of love overcame the distractions that sought to penetrate my fortress.

I really was at one with myself and nothing could have distracted me.

I was at peace in the hands of love.

Yes, it must have been love to create such unity within me.

Indeed the lovers who were in the train whispered to each other in perfect harmony, unaware of what was going on around them.

I whispered to my God whom I had rediscovered.

'Poustinia.'

To create the desert in crowded places.

To make a railway carriage a place of meditation, to make the streets of my city into the corridors of my ideal convent.

*   *   *

I shall tell you something else which is very important for busy people like you who say they have no time to pray.

Try to look at the reality in which you live – your work, your commitments, your relationships, your meetings, your walks, the shopping, the newspapers, the children – as a single whole from which you cannot disengage yourself, a whole which you have to think about.

I shall say more: a whole by means of which God speaks to you and through which He guides you.

So it is not by fleeing that you will find God more easily, but it is by changing your heart that you will see things differently.

The desert in the city is only possible on these terms: that you see things with a new eye, touch them with a new spirit, love them with a new heart.

Teilhard de Chardin would say: embrace them with a pure heart.

So there is no need to flee, to alienate yourself, to get caught up between dream and reality, torn between what you think and what you do, no need to go and pray and then kill yourself with work, to swing back and forth between Martha and Mary, to be permanently in chaos, to have a divided heart, not to know where to lay your head.

Yes, reality is highly instructive!

Reality is the true vehicle in which God moves towards us.

I find God more vitally in reality than in the fine thoughts I weave around Him.

Especially if the reality is painful and my will is put to a harsh test, especially if I rediscover my inadequacy.

★   ★   ★

Let me tell you what happened to me in this connection.

When I left for the desert I left everything behind me as Jesus had asked me to – I left family, house, money, situation. The only thing I didn't leave were my ideas about God which were all packed into a big book about theology, and this book I took with me.

And there on the sand I went on reading and re-reading this book as if God were contained in an idea and as if I could communicate with Him because I had fine ideas about Him.

My novice-master said to me, 'Brother Carlo, leave those books alone. Put yourself stripped and humble in front of the Eucharist. Empty yourself, de-intellectualize yourself, try to love, try to contemplate . . . .'.

But I didn't understand a word of what he was trying to say to me. I remained thoroughly anchored to my ideas.

So he thought it would help me to empty myself, and to understand, if he sent me to work.

My goodness!

It isn't easy to work in those oases in the heat of the day!

When I returned to the fraternity I felt absolutely whacked, all my strength drained out of me.

I collapsed onto the matting in front of the Sacrament in the chapel, my head aching, my back breaking. And all my ideas flew away like birds flying from an open cage.

I couldn't even start to pray. I was arid, empty, exhausted. The only thing that came from my mouth was a groan.

The only positive thing that I felt, and that I began to understand, was solidarity with the poor, the truly poor, with anyone crushed under the weight of the daily yoke, with anyone on the assembly line. And I thought of my mother praying with five children around her feet, and of the peasants who had to work a twelve hour day in the summer.

If peace and quiet were a prerequisite of prayer, then those poor people wouldn't have ever been able to pray. So evidently the prayer I had abundantly practised up till then was the prayer of the rich, the prayer of comfortable well-fed people who were masters of their own timetable.

I no longer understood anything, or rather I was beginning to understand a great deal.

I wept!

My tears fell on the overall that was a mark of my poor man's toil.

And it was in that state of authentic poverty that I made the most important discovery of my life of prayer.

Do you want to know what it was?

That prayer takes place in the heart, not in the head.

I felt as if a vein were opening in my heart and for the first time I 'experienced' a new dimension of the union with God.

What an extraordinary adventure I was embarking on.

I shall never forget that moment.

I was like an olive crushed in the press.

Yet over and above the oppression, it was unspeakably sweet to feel the reality in which I was living sweeping over me.

I was in total peace. The pain accepted in love was like a gateway enabling me to pass beyond mere things.

I intuited the stability of God. Since that time I have always thought that that was contemplative prayer.

The gift that God makes of Himself to whoever offers Him his life, as the Gospel says: 'He who loses his life for my sake will find it' (*Matthew 10:39*).

★   ★   ★

So now, courage!

Choose a week to do your 'poustinia'; that is to say, choose a week to find the desert in the heart of the city and in the midst of your commitments.

Have your Bible near you.

You will find in what follows a theme for each day, one that you can develop with the help of the biblical references.

I have also chosen the psalms and the readings you should use for your morning and evening prayer.

On one of these days you will go to confession to a priest.

Try to finish your retreat with the memorial of the death and resurrection of Jesus which is the Lord's day, Sunday, take part in the Eucharistic liturgy and receive the body and blood of Jesus in Holy Communion.

★   ★   ★

If you want your desert in the city to yield immediate and tangible fruit, then spend an hour in contemplative prayer every night, placing your body, too, in a praying attitude.

24

THE PRESENCE
OF GOD

Monday

The theme for today is the presence of God, His presence within ourselves, within nature, within history.

I propose that you should nourish your prayer with the following biblical texts and with the following daily pattern.

LAUDS   Psalm 94
(Morning   Psalm 139
   Prayer)   David's canticle (*I Chronicles 22*)

VESPERS   Psalm 46
(Evening   Psalm 104
   Prayer)   The Vision of the Lamb (*Apocalypse 3 and 5*)

READINGS   Genesis 1
            Isaiah 59
            John 1

★   ★   ★

I don't know how it happened to you, but I know how it happened to me.

God arrived in my heart like a huge parable. Everything around me spoke to me of Him.

The sky spoke to me of Him,
the earth spoke to me of Him,
the sea spoke to me of Him.
He was like a secret hidden in all things, visible and invisible.

He was like the solution to all problems.

He was like the most important Person who had ever entered my life and with whom I should have lived for ever.

Very soon I felt myself enveloped by Him as a 'Presence always Present', one who looked at me from all the leaves of the wood I was walking through, and across the clouds riding briskly along the sky above my head.

I have never had any difficulty in feeling God's presence, especially when I was small. Rather, His absence would have seemed very strange and very unlikely.

I felt myself to be in God
like a bird in the air
like a log in the fire
like a baby in its mother's womb.

This last image was the strongest, the truest, and it is always growing.

I truly think that a woman's womb containing a baby is the theme of the whole universe, the visibility of invisible things, the sign of the way God works in order to make me His son.

In Him I live and breathe, and I rejoice in His Presence as creator, even if – and I suffer for it – the time has not yet come for me to see his divine countenance, as the Bible says, 'face to face' (*I Corinthians 13: 12*).

It is early yet.

*   *   *

This experience of God's presence in all things and in every situation is not only mine, it belongs to the People of God, that is to say to those who believe, the children of Abraham, as the Bible calls them.

This is how Psalm 139 expresses the authentic experience of a people that has questioned itself throughout the centuries of its history:

> O Lord, thou has searched me and known me!
> Thou knowest when I sit down and when I rise up;
> thou discernest my thoughts from afar.
> Thou searchest out my path and my lying down . . .

and it continues with a marvellous crescendo:

> Whither shall I go from thy Spirit?
> Or whither shall I flee from thy presence?
> If I ascend to heaven, thou art there,
> If I make my bed in Sheol, thou art there!
> If I take the wings of the morning
> and dwell in the uttermost parts of the sea,
> even there thy hand shall lead me,
> and thy right hand shall hold me.
> If I say, 'Let only darkness cover me,
> and the light about me be night',
> even the darkness is not dark to thee,
> the night is bright as the day;
> for darkness is as light with thee.

★　　★　　★

The experience of God's presence in nature and in history for me is fundamental.

It is the substance of faith.

Gradually I must arrive at living it, at feeling it by day and by night, being aware of it when I work and when I rest, enjoying it when I pray and when I love.

Always!

Twenty-four hours out of twenty-four!

It is the path that leads me to live in the Kingdom of God which is the union between heaven and earth, between God and man.

But let us understand each other: it is not a matter of establishing the union with God on our side. Because that union exists; it already existed before I was aware of it.

That is an absolute because nothing exists outside God.

In God 'we live and move and have our being' (*Acts 17: 28*); this is the basis of all reality, the explanation of Being, the very significance of Life, the enduring root of Love.

What matters on our side is to become aware of this union, to be attentive to it in faith, to deepen it in hope, to live it in charity.

It is the story of the baby who gradually discovers its mother and father, of the woman who finds her husband, of the man who finds a friend.

But the mother and father were there already, the husband was there already, the friend was there already.

And God was there already. It is for us to discover Him within ourselves, not to create Him.

God's presence in ourselves, in the Cosmos, in the Invisible, in Everything, is basic. You will never be in any place, in any situation, where He is not.

> O Lord thou hast searched me and known me!
> Thou knowest when I sit down and when I rise up;
> thou discoverest my thoughts from afar,
> Thou searchest out my path and my lying down . . .

And it is silly to think that He is in church and not in the street, that He is in the Sacrament and not in the crowd, that He is in happiness and not in sorrow, in bright kind things and not in storms and earthquakes.

★   ★   ★

God is always there.

I have arrived at the state of being aware of Him always and everywhere, and this is my strength as John says: 'And this is the victory that overcomes the world, our faith' (*I John 5: 4*).

I see Him at the root of everything, at the base of every happening, in the transparency of every truth, in the storehouse of every love.

Always!

And it is because of this that I am happy.

And that I never feel lonely.

The great thing I owe to Him as Presence is that He has removed all my fears, and by healing all the complexes that beset me He has given me an absolute sense of 'liberation', a sense that increases every day.

Ever since I feared Him, I have not been afraid of anyone.

But my fear of Him is not a servile fear, it is the sweetest fear, the fear a child has of a fantastic father who has told him an infinitude of things but is concealing another infinitude.

In other words, my fear is linked to His 'Mystery'.

But I do not mind this because it means that every day, as I converse with Him, there is always a great pile of news, because nothing is so full of news as mystery.

And the pile is never exhausted.

★   ★   ★

Yes, God is present in my life, present in history, present in events, present in nature, present in everything that is.

This signifies belief in God, hope in God, love for God.

The temptation that can arise from our cultural past, indeed from the infancy of mankind, is to think anthropomorphically of God, to see Him as an old man on a white cloud, or as an eye in an equilateral triangle, and I have never appreciated better than now the importance of the recommendation in Deuteronomy:

> Beware lest you act corruptly by making a graven image for yourselves, in the form of any figure, the likeness of male or female, the likeness of any beast that is on the earth, the likeness of any winged bird that flies in the air, the likeness of anything that creeps on the ground (*Deuteronomy 4: 16–18*).

> Since you saw no form on the day that the Lord spoke to you at the Horeb out of the midst of the fire (*Deuteronomy 4: 15*).

★   ★   ★

If the transcendence of God is to reach me it is not going to pass through a likeness that deforms Him. No, it is announced by a Sign that shows it as beauty, as the house and the banquet, as heaven and earth.

And the sign does not take possession of the Presence, it never orchestrates it, it has no power to limit it.

It is a sign, only a sign, extraordinarily transparent.

But the presence goes beyond the sign as my life goes beyond my body and my desires go beyond my potentialities.

God's presence is in the substance of the Cosmos, in the substance of man, in the substance of history. It does not go before, it is within, though being within does not in any way condition it, because, as it is transcendent, it is never identified with its container. Just as my person is not limited by my body in which it lives but, like a mystery, always goes over and beyond it and infinitely outstrips it.

Yes, the mystery of God is the mystery of the Person and, in last analysis, we who are created 'in His own image' (*Genesis 1: 27*) follow in His traces.

God is immanent in the Cosmos and at the same time He is transcendent to it.

The mystery of the Trinity is the mystery of the Transcendence of God that can never be conditioned by the unicity of His Nature. What liberates from conditioning is Love.

Life, which is the Father, says to Light which is the Son: 'I love you.'

From this statement and from the rejoinder, 'I love you too', proceeds Love which is the Holy Spirit.

And communication is made.

★ ★ ★

What makes the communication is Love. And indeed it is through love that you emerge from solitude.

So long as you do not love you remain in the staticity of your Nature. As soon as Love falls upon you, you wake up and become aware of the Other.

The Other in an absolute sense is God and substitutes itself (without eliminating them, rather by harmonizing with them) for all the Others which in your experience set out towards you: matter and spirit, emotion and reason, joy and sorrow, the visible and the invisible, earth and heaven, time and eternity, beauty and logic, the house and the Kingdom, death and resurrection.

God is truly everything, the reason for everything, the key to everything.

To believe in Him means to see everything as the Living One who watches you from all the points of his Being and embraces you as His beloved son.

To believe in God means light, peace, joy, exultation.
Not to believe means darkness, sorrow, staticity, death.

*　　*　　*

The communication between myself and God is basic, like
the communication between the fœtus and the womb that
contains it.

The fœtus is me. The womb is the whole universe in its living
fruitfulness and in the dynamic of evolution which is history.

I feel myself watched by God through the light that surrounds
me and the stars that are above me; I feel myself touched by Him
in the wind that reaches me, the water that wets me, the hunger
that stimulates me, the matter that collides with me and wounds
me.

I feel that He begets me through the crock full of bread, the
friend who talks to me, the grief that makes me cry, the joy that
delights me.

I am never outside of Him, far from Him, without Him.

If praying means 'being in God', then I can say that I pray
everywhere because everywhere is His temple.

To say, 'I can't pray because I've got work to do' is absurd.

Who is stopping you from praying while you work? Isn't it
better to believe that while working you can be at prayer?

Why reduce prayer to word, thought, place, time?

Go beyond all that.

If by prayer you understand communicating with a Presence,
and if this Presence is everywhere, then you can always be at
prayer.

If only to communicate.

And to communicate means to love.

It is in loving that you pray, because it is love that carries you to the loved person, and you can love through talking, crying, thinking, walking, sleeping, always, always, always. Twenty-four hours out of twenty-four.

★　★　★

We need to let ourselves be 'tempted' by a sense of God's immanence, a sense that sees God everywhere, God in things, God in nature, God 'in every place', as Pius X's catechism put it. Do not be afraid of exaggerating.

Christian personalism, the reality of Transcendence and the contemplation of the Trinity will steer you away from the dangers of immanence and its immobility and will make you exclaim: 'Our Father who art in heaven!' The dynamic of these concepts will always bring you back to the fullness of the revelation of Jesus.

Yet we need to start off with the experience of God in nature, God in the encounter with men in scientific research, God in social commitment, in physical phenomena, in the splendour of a sunset, in the might of the sea, in the grain of wheat that dies.

Modern atheism has fed too much on our infantile medieval piety where everything was transcendence and even the Incarnation was afraid of men's bodies and the dynamic of evolution.

That is why the university faculties most dangerous to faith have become those of medicine, physics, chemistry and biology – that is to say those most intimately concerned with created things, with matter.

But the day is at hand when we shall have rediscovered a new idiom, and the Spirit will breathe over scientific researchers as violently as it breathed over Teilhard de Chardin in the desert when he touched the stone slab on which he had laid his head in a night alive and full with the presence of God – and he experienced matter. Then they will start to sing a hymn to matter, as he did, rather as if it were a mature comment from the modern world on the Book of Genesis.

T. de Chardin:

Blessed be you, harsh matter, barren soil, stubborn rock: you who yield only to violence, you who force us to work if we would eat.

Blessed be you, perilous matter, violent sea, untameable passion: you who unless we fetter you will devour us. . .

Blessed be you, universal matter, immeasurable time, boundless ether, triple abyss of stars and atoms and generations: you who by overflowing and dissolving our narrow standards of measurement reveal to us the dimensions of God.

Blessed be you, impenetrable matter: you who, interposed between our minds and the world of essences, cause us to languish with the desire to pierce through the seamless veil of phenomena.

Blessed be you, mortal matter: you who one day will undergo the process of dissolution within us and will thereby take us forcibly into the very heart of that which exists.

Without you, without your onslaughts, without your uprootings of us, we should remain all our lives inert, stagnant, puerile, ignorant both of ourselves and of God. You who batter us and then dress our wounds, you who resist us and yield to us, you who wreck and build, you who shackle and liberate, the sap of our souls, the hand of God, the flesh of Christ: it is you, matter, that I bless. . .

I acclaim you as the melodious fountain of water whence spring the souls of men and as the limpid crystal whereof is fashioned the New Jerusalem.

I acclaim you as the divine *milieu*, charged with creative

power, as the ocean stirred by the Spirit, as the clay moulded
and infused with life by the incarnate Word.[3]

*   *   *

Yes, between modern atheism and faith there is now only a thin
veil. I have felt it in myself and with what delight have I torn it
away.

Now I feel one
One with myself
One with my brothers
One with nature
One with the galaxies
One with God.

And now I am happy because to be one with the One-in-All is
the source of the deepest human joy.

If the All is One, if the infinite multiplicity of things may be
brought back to the Unity of the divine Being, then it means that
all things are ruled by Love which is God Himself, and that the
present situation of war and selfishness and darkness will come to
an end with man's maturity, with man redeemed and saved.

If the All is One it means that peace is already on the way, that
the banquet in my house is the sign of a universal banquet that
Jesus has called Kingdom – that is to say 'God with us' – where all
mankind will find its happiness, and history its harmonious victory
over chaos.

*   *   *

You asked me, brother, to help you find God in the city, to help
you live your desert in the asphalt jungle where you spend your
days, to help you feel His presence exactly where you are.

[3] Teilhard de Chardin, *Hymn of the Universe*, Harper & Row, New York, 1965,
and Fount Paperbacks, London, 1970.

I have met your wishes.

I have left you at your home.

I have shown you that the things that you see, the situation in which you live, are God's 'place', the 'context' of His presence, the way-of-being His logic demands. I have shown you His hands touching you, the fruitful reality He is making of you.

Now put yourself in front of your largest window, go up to the one whence your eye can command the greatest number of things, then kneel down in the humility of your heart and greet the day with me:

Come, Holy Spirit,
send us from heaven
a ray of your light.
Come, father of the poor,
come, bestower of gifts,
come, light of our hearts.
You are the perfect consoler,
sweet guest of the soul,
most gentle refreshment.
You are repose in our toil,
coolness in our heat,
comfort in our tears.
O most blessed light,
invade our hearts,
for without your strength,
there is nothing in man.
Wash what is soiled,
bathe what is parched,
heal what is bleeding.
Bend what is rigid,
melt what is frozen,

straighten what is crooked.
Give to your faithful
who trust in you alone
your holy gifts.
Give virtue and rewards,
give us a holy death,
give us eternal joy.

Amen.

EVERYTHING
IS A SIGN OF HIM

Tuesday

Everything is a sign of God. There is no place that is empty of His presence. I must accustom myself to this idea so as to re-inforce the desert in the city and fill it with His love.

LAUDS	Psalm 42
(Morning	Psalm 18
Prayer)	Sirach's song (*42 and 43*)
VESPERS	Psalm 16
(Evening	Psalm 130
Prayer)	Zechariah's hymn (*Luke 1*)
READINGS	Exodus 16
	Colossians (*all*)
	John 13

★　　★　　★

God is present in everything and everything is a sign of Him. Just as my visible body is the sign of my person and indicates it, so everything visible and invisible is the sign of God and proclaims Him continually and inexorably.

There is not a cell, there is not an atom, there is not the smallest detail that can escape from the unity of the whole which the signs indicate with inexorable logic, harmony and unity.

The signs have told me my history, have explained my desires, have shed light on my questions.

The sign of a bird's nest or a fox's lair has synthesized for me the soul of the whole universe, and Newton's law on the attraction of the stars has prepared me for the opening verses of St John's Gospel.

The logic of a chemical combination has exemplified for me the interdependence between men and things, while the impenetrability of bodies has attested to the scope of my freedom.

But where the sign becomes a constant point of reference, an unequivocal indication of what it wants to indicate and proclaim, is when it indicates and proclaims another Presence in myself.

Everything I see, every noise I hear, every dawn that returns, every encounter I achieve, are signs of something or someone who has gone before me and questions me:

God.

Of course I can always say, 'I don't believe in Him'.

There is in me – and it is my most real sin – the power of not believing, the power of saying No to hope, the capability of not wanting to love . . . and yet you can be sure of this: the sign will not cease to question me even if it has to wait till the end of time.

In my folly I can say: 'I've not got your cards of identity, I don't believe you, you were probably born as a result of spontaneous generation, you made yourself by yourself, you're the result of chance', but this is certainly not the way by which I achieve peace and joy.

At the most I can achieve a certain calm, a touch of melancholy and an arid indifference.

Rejoicing and happiness will never be mine and I shall never know a marriage of love.

★　　★　　★

In order to understand the signs that you see and perceive their significance you must be small and humble of heart.

It is essential!

It seems absurd but it is precisely for this reason that many people remain outside the truth. 'Seeing they do not see, and hearing they do not hear . . .' (*Matthew 13: 13*).

And God passes them by.

To Jesus this situation is very serious and He has threatening words to say: 'Unless you turn and become like children, you will never enter the Kingdom' (*Matthew 18: 3*).

Have you understood?

You will never enter!

To enter the Kingdom signifies, as a beginning, to understand things, to be attentive to what the Invisible Presence is saying to you by means of the infinity of signs in which you are immersed

like a drop in the ocean

like a leaf in the wood

like an ant on a mountain.

But in order to enter, in order to understand, it is necessary to have a child's heart.

You must ask for it.

How can you understand with the help of your intelligence alone?

The mystery of God has its seat in man's heart, and even if it starts making itself felt in his brain, he still finds the answer only in love.

It is by loving that you understand.

Communication is Love.

The sign is explained, interpreted, understood in love.

You see your home and, in love, it becomes the sign of another home which is Paradise.

You see a wedding feast and this becomes, for the people of God who know how to love, the sign of another Wedding Feast in which is proclaimed the intimacy between God and man.

For those who love, time becomes the counterpoint of eternity, as space becomes the first letter in the alphabet of 'non-space'; the visible becomes the ideal context for the Invisible, and war and violence catalyse in the heart the dream of universal peace.

Death puts depth into the first interrogation concerning a God who renews all things and has the power to raise His son from the dead.

★　★　★

Don't be afraid, brother.

I know it is difficult to believe, but I assure you that it is more difficult not to believe.

Try very hard to have a child's heart and a child's eyes, then everything will be easier for you.

Gaze at things, study things; don't be afraid of wasting time strolling along by the sea or looking in a microscope at the harmonious structure of the infinitely small.

It is precisely in those signs, there in front of you, that your intuition of God and your faith in God are born, and it is not for nothing, not by chance, that they are looking at you.

You must not believe that it is only you who look at things, try to believe that things look at you. God looks at you through all the lights of the city where you walk at night, and from all the clouds that pass like flocks of sheep over your head.

God embraces you through the wind that blows back your hair and He kisses you with the first rays of the morning sun.

The tools of your daily work can be the touch of God's hands, and His greeting the whistle of the train that passes over the viaduct by your house.

If you do not want the signs of creation all around you to distract you, then fill them with the presence of God.

They will speak to you of Him. If you want the streets that you pace to become the corridors of your favourite convent, then see them in the light of His presence.

Your work will no longer be a burden, separating you from prayer, if you carry it out as an act of obedience to His Word resounding in your ears:

'In the sweat of your face you shall eat bread' (*Genesis 3: 19*).

And men, with their infinite contradictions, will cease to be instruments of distraction if you try to see them as Jesus saw them and feel for them as He felt for them:

'I have compassion on the crowd' (*Mark 8: 2*).

God's presence which comes to you by means of signs will transform the environment where you live into a temple where you will be able 'to worship God in spirit and in truth' (*John 4: 24*).

How can there be a more living desert than yours if you see it as inhabited by the Living God?

★   ★   ★

But now we must take a step forward.

God's presence coming to you by means of signs is only the first step.

Poor us if God had stopped there!

We would still be in the garden of Eden, looking for Him

beneath the trees and having Him as our good neighbour.

A great deal has happened since then under the thrust of a love as radical as God's!

God did not intend us to be His neighbours – He called us to be His sons. He is not satisfied with greeting us with 'good morning' but takes on Himself our sufferings and limitations to the point of dying for us.

He does not offer us a meeting of ideas or of devotional prayers but a blood alliance.

We are utterly bowled over by the amplitude of His design over us!

I am tempted to think that we ought to learn to believe what He tells us a little at a time, because if we believed His word truly and all at once we would go mad with joy.

But let us return to the concept of presence.

God's presence in things, in history, in me, is a vital presence.

By loving me God begets me and makes me His son.

His presence in me is a generative presence.

However there are two periods in this generative process.

There is the initial unconscious period of Genesis in which the Spirit 'is moving over the waters' and creates without asking my permission – He makes me earth, a bit of a star, a flower of the field, a harmonious animal – and there is the period which is 'the maturity of years' when, as with Mary, the Spirit 'overshadows me' and asks me for my 'Yes'.

Having to make me a son in His image, He makes me free; desiring me to enter the intimacy of His family, He gives me the possibility of running away from home.

The mystery of our freedom springs from the greatness of His love, for there is no true and great love without freedom.

God wants our love for Him to be free, because love is an absolute.

And absolutes are not imposed.

Even God cannot force me to love Him.

This is why His offer is always an offer that calls for alliance, and why in its fullness the Gospel likes to give it the name of Kingdom.

'The Kingdom of Heaven is at hand' announces John the Baptist (*Matthew 3: 2*). 'The Kingdom of God has come upon you' confirms Jesus (*Matthew 12: 28*).

★　★　★

The Kingdom of God . . . is God with us.

It is the news that God has pitched His tent among us.

And it is such joyful news that it came to be called the Good News.

Here is a summary of the Gospel that was announced to men, a statement capable of turning our lives upside down with its significance.

St John sums up the announcement in the famous opening verses of his Gospel which alone are enough to make us rejoice:

> In the beginning was the Word
> and the Word was with God,
> and the Word was God.
> He was in the beginning with God;
> all things were made through him,
> and without him was not anything made
> that was made.
> In him was life,
> and the life was the light of men.
> The light shines in the darkness,
> and the darkness has not overcome it. . . .
> He was in the world,

and the world was made through him,
yet the world knew him not.
He came to his own home,
and his own people received him not.
But to all who received him,
who believed in his name,
he gave power to become
children of God;
who were born, not of blood
nor of the will of the flesh
nor of the will of man,
but of God.
And the word became flesh
and dwelt among us,
full of grace and truth;
we have beheld his glory,
glory as of the only Son from the Father (*John 1*).

★   ★   ★

From henceforth the story of the earth is the story of heaven.
God and man are bound together in a single destiny.
The concerns of man are the concerns of God.
The homes of man are the homes of God.
One single Kingdom receives God and man: the Kingdom of
Heaven.

★   ★   ★

The Kingdom into which God has 'delivered us from the
dominion of darkness' (*Colossians 1: 13*) is called the Kingdom of
Heaven.

From this definition I understand that it is a hidden Kingdom, because heaven means hidden.[4]

It is an important indication. As a man and as a citizen of the earth I belong to a state and own its passport; at the same time I have another passport in my pocket, that of the Kingdom of Heaven.

It is as if I am a partisan who operates in a country as yet unconquered but who intends to conquer it.

If I am serious about it I shall soon realize that I have enemies. Indeed it is already obvious that the totalitarian and ideologized regimes will not be able to tolerate me, and if they discover me they will try to eliminate me or stand in my way.

But I myself have no intention of eliminating anyone if only because on my passport as follower of Christ there is written:

'Blessed are the merciful',

'Blessed are the peacemakers',

not to mention the downright:

'Blessed are the persecuted'.

What a strange Kingdom!

Who can understand it?

What is clear in the concept of this Kingdom is that it begins today, it begins from my conversion, it does not wait for my death to get me going.

Today!

It is a Kingdom today.

I must act today.

I know it is a Kingdom that will have no end, that will bestride the frontier of death itself, that will grow immeasurably bigger outside time, that is 'escatological' as we like to say among ourselves, but that is already among us and should commit us to all its consequences.

---

[4] A concept with an etymological foundation in the original Italian which is akin to the Latin *caelum* (sky) and *caelatum* (hidden). [Tr.]

Diognetus knew better than anyone how to sum up the Christian's position as a partisan of the Kingdom of Heaven while living in the climate of the Roman Empire.

And not for nothing did the Romans get the impression that the Christians would have overthrown the Empire. But the Christians themselves were thinking quite other thoughts as Diognetus pointed out:

> Christians do not distinguish themselves from other men by their country, their language or their dress.
>
> They do not belong to any particular city, they do not make use of special dialects, their way of life has nothing particular about it.
>
> They do not set themselves up, as many others do, as champions of a human doctrine.
>
> They do not distribute themselves in Greek or barbaric cities according to pre-arranged divisions.
>
> They conform to local customs as regards clothes, food and life-style while bearing witness to the extraordinary and truly paradoxical laws of the spiritual republic to which they belong.
>
> They live each in his own country but like strangers in the house.
>
> They fulfil all their duties as citizens, and put up with all their tasks, but like strangers.
>
> Every strange land is their country and every country is for them a strange land.
>
> In the same way they are in the flesh but they do not live according to the flesh.

★　★　★

Now I shall explain to you, with an example, how recruitment for the Kingdom of Heaven is carried out.

Luke tells us about it in Chapter 19 of his Gospel:

> [Jesus] entered Jericho and was passing through. And there was a man named Zacchaeus; he was a chief tax collector, and rich. And he sought to see who Jesus was, but could not, on account of the crowd, because he was small of stature. So he ran on ahead and climbed up into a sycamore tree to see him, for he was to pass that way. And when Jesus came to the place, he looked up and said to him, 'Zacchaeus, make haste and come down; for I must stay at your house today.' So he made haste and came down, and received him joyfully. And when they saw it they all murmured, 'he has gone in to be a guest of a man who is a sinner.' And Zaccheus stood and said to the Lord, 'Behold, Lord, the half of my goods I give to the poor; and if I have defrauded anyone of anything, I restore it fourfold.' And Jesus said to him, 'Today salvation has come to this house, since he also is a son of Abraham. For the Son of man came to seek and to save the lost' (*Luke 19: 1–10*).

★　　★　　★

And Zacchaeus was recruited. Henceforth he had the living experience of what the Kingdom of Heaven is. He understood who was its King, he understood what the King wanted, he had heard the call in the depths of his being and had responded with courage.

In that encounter between God's call and the practical acceptance of it, between the requirement to be poor ('blessed are the poor') and the practical dispossession ('the half of my goods I give to the poor'), there lies the 'happening'.

The Kingdom of Heaven is not polite chatter, idle talk, a vague promise, it is an act, it is the encounter between two serious and genuine wills, it is a conversion to light, to love and to life itself, because God is Light, Love and Life.

*　　*　　*

So you see how far we are from the Kingdom of Heaven!
It's terrifying to think of it.
Our distance is marked by talk, only talk, always talk.
And what use is it?
It was Jesus who said: 'Not everyone who says to me "Lord, Lord," shall enter the Kingdom of Heaven, but he who does the will of my Father' (*Matthew 7: 21*).
If we want to enter we must 'act' not 'talk'.
God asks us for the commitment of our whole being.
It is a real and continuous conversion.
In the Kingdom it is deeds that count.

*　　*　　*

There is, however, a fact that is not a deed yet bestows the right of citizenship in the Kingdom of Heaven. This is 'the poor man's longing'.
And it is as vast as the sea
As beautiful as light
As glowing as fire.
The poor man's longing is man's painful striving after a dream that is greater than himself.
This longing occurs when God dwells in a man and transmits His warmth to him.
Into the weakness and limitations of a poor man there enters the longing for God.
It is then that, imprisoned in bed by sickness, you travel

throughout the wide world, and, humiliated by your sin, you languish behind dreams of light and holiness.

There is no limit to the poor man's longing when He broaches the Beatitudes of the Lord of Life.

It is in this longing that He succeeds in identifying more closely with Life itself, in penetrating its Light and in anticipating its Love on this earth.

Most men do not succeed in fulfilling themselves in action on this earth.

Whether through weakness, whether through poverty, whether through ignorance, they founder on the path of action. Defeated, humiliated and unemployed, they have nothing to do but weep.

But if, after the weeping and after the affliction, they succeed in understanding who God is and what He wants to make of them and their poverty, they will discover the greatest secret of life and of the Kingdom: and this is that, in God's eyes, doing or not doing, succeeding or not succeeding, are not the point; what matters is loving.

And if my love has not been realized in action, then it is realizing itself today in my poor man's longing.

And if my love has not been realized in marriage, then it is realizing itself in celibacy.

There is no limit to longing, and we can truly say:

We are our longings.

I have what I longed for.

In action I have discovered my limitations and my impotence, in longing, in desire, I have realized my true dream; in the actual I have understood the earth, in desire I have intuited the Kingdom.

Woe to us if the Kingdom of God were the outcome of everyone's action. Apart from being an injustice – because in that case it would be the heritage of the strong, the intelligent, the competent and the clever – it would be a very small thing.

No, the Kingdom of God is the outcome of a huge longing, a huge desire, born in the poor man's heart and transferred into the pierced heart of the Poor Man *par excellence*: Christ.

THE KINGDOM WHERE
LOVE REIGNS

Wednesday

The Kingdom of Heaven signifies God with us. There could be no more exalting news for us. God is with me vitally – God is united to me. My life becomes divine life, my history sacred history.

LAUDS	Psalm 23
(Morning	Psalm 122
prayer)	Tobit's song of praise (*13*)
VESPERS	Psalm 8
(Evening	Psalm 126
Prayer)	Marriage hymn (*Apocalypse 19*)
READINGS	Ezekiel 36
	Hosea 2
	Luke 13

★   ★   ★

Yesterday we talked about the Kingdom of Heaven, this hidden Kingdom, this concealed Kingdom to which faith has made me assent, to which hope has drawn me, and which charity reveals as being the Kingdom of truth and life, the Kingdom of light and love, the Kingdom of justice and peace.

It is a Kingdom that has been prepared for us 'since the foundation of the world' (*Matthew 25: 34*) and which unfolds without 'signs to be observed' (*Luke 17: 20*). It is a Kingdom into which Christ has transferred us, delivering us from the 'dominion of darkness' (*Colossians 1: 12*) and into which 'it is hard for those who have riches to enter' (*Luke 18: 24*).

It is a Kingdom where 'he who is least is greater than John [the Baptist]' (*Luke 7: 28*) and where our 'names are written in heaven' (*Luke 10: 20*).

It is a Kingdom which was like a grain of mustard seed at first, and then 'it grew and became a tree, and the birds of the air made nests in its branches' (*Luke 13: 19*) and where 'men will come from east and west, and from north and south, and sit at table' (*Luke 13: 29*).

All this we know from the Gospel. But we also know that the Kingdom is more than a place or a legislative entity, it is a Person: Jesus.

It is His unique characteristic.

The point of convergence of my faith, the strength of my hope, the driving force of my love is a Person: Christ.

The threads of the perfect revolution are held by Him, the centre of every assembly is Him.

He is counsellor.

He is consoler.

It's a marvellous way of facilitating things.

It's the simplest way of developing the dynamic of love in that it is always a relationship between two people.

I–you.

And in this 'you' there is God who has pitched His tent beside me and is called Jesus.

★   ★   ★

The Lord is my shepherd,
I shall not want;
he makes me lie down in green pastures,
he leads me beside still waters;
he restores my soul (*Psalm 23*).

To believe that God is my shepherd, that He leads me, that He calls me by name, gives me great security and great tenderness.

My weakness comes from feeling that I am alone in the great city.

It is when I cannot understand things, when I suffer, when I cry, when the experience of my limitations throws me against the wall of my incapacity, when my poverty, my inadequacy, makes me understand what it is to be a man – it is then that I must make the leap into hope and believe in the God of the Impossible.

But what do I do instead?

Too often I withdraw into myself and forget what I have told Him in my prayers:

'Lord you are my shepherd.'

And I forget it just when I need to remember it most.

We do not travel life's journey alone – this should be the constant thought of my faith.

We can count on God and in a very practical way.

It is He who can help us.

If a baby, needing to come out of his mother's womb, depended only on his own strength and skill, he would never see the light.

But there is someone who will help him out.

It is the very dynamic of nature, it is the mystery of what has gone before, it is the generating process in which he is immersed, that will help him to come out of the waters.

Our weakness is that we look at ourselves, always at ourselves, only at ourselves.

We do not realize that our mother is at hand and that God is the mother in whom we live and have our being.

And that He will bring us out into the light.

★   ★   ★

The Kingdom of Heaven signifies God with us.

In messianic times this truth is announced and made possible by the will of God.

It is the essence of the Gospels, the good news to the poor.

And who are the poor?

I am the poor, God's child in the womb of the dark generating process, who cries out his limitations and incapacity.

Now I have been told about Him and am aware of Him.

Today He has been announced.

The reality existed before, but I was not ready to receive it and so it did not count.

God says nothing to me if I do not perceive that He is alive.

It is no use for Him to come to me if I do not see Him.

Messianic times are linked to a maturity of faith. Messianic times did not come suddenly. They did not come at the beginning of the story of Adam nor did they come at the beginning of my life. They came when man was able to understand, when I was able to understand.

Messianic times are the times of love, that is to say the moment when I notice the other, God.

The times that go before prepare for the coming, messianic times are the coming itself.

They are the today of love,

the today of communication.

They are life just for two.

They are the start of my sacred history.

My sacred history starts from the moment when I experience in faith that I am not alone any more, that henceforth I shall travel with Him.

And fear is at an end.

★   ★   ★

There are just the two of us.

He is the king, I am His subject, and together we forge and develop the Kingdom.

But there are the two of us.

And he is the more important, I have to admit.

It seems absurd to say this, but the truth is that men regard themselves as being more important than God, they feel that it is they who are at the centre of things and events.

Only a few people put God at the centre of things and events and look at him with the eye of faith.

In order that we may all arrive at this state, truth offers us poverty, weakness and sin as props to help us, but we are so steeped in pride that most people do not believe until they have been reduced to shreds.

Not for nothing is humility the queen of the virtues and it is only through her that we can approach God.

We take a huge step forward in our approach when we experience in faith that our history is not forged by ourselves alone. We forge it with Him.

And He is the first and we are the second.

My vocation is in His hands before it is in my own hands.

My future lies with Him.

Girls sink into depression when they reach a certain age because they cannot see what the future holds.

The worry that they may not fulfil themselves, that they may not marry, paralyses them, and for some it becomes a tragedy.

And the more they suffer, the more they withdraw into themselves. The more they need space, the more they retreat within narrow horizons.

Whereas if they could manage to fix their eyes on God in faith, and see Him as their neighbour, their ally, their king, their friend, their brother, their father, they would cease to beat their heads against an unknown destiny and begin to perceive the truth of a vocation more difficult but deeper, more demanding but truer.

Each of us has his own path to tread and it is more beautiful if it is offered by God. It is foolishness to want another one, and we incur pointless suffering if we insist on things that do not exist or on paths not made for us.

To accept the Kingdom of Heaven within us means to accept the vocation that God prepares for us through the reality in which we live.

★   ★   ★

But God goes before me.

And He is God because He has gone before everyone ever since the creation.

He went before Adam.

He went before Abraham.

He went before David.

He went before Moses.

And it is He who gives everyone his particular vocation.

He called Adam into life, He brought Abraham out of his country, He taught David to sing, He gave Moses the power to lead.

And in order to make them understand that it was He Himself who was acting, calling, bringing to life, He led them to the limit of their poverty.

For Adam this was represented by man's weakness, for Abraham by Sarah's barrenness, for David by the humiliation he endured in his horrible sin, for Moses by the impassability of the Red Sea and the continuing 'murmuring' of his people.

God always leads man to his limit so that he may understand and enjoy the Good News – and the extreme limit is death which no one can escape.

The Good News is this: that God is God, that God is the God of the Impossible, He is the God who can make Sarah's barren womb fruitful and separate the waters of the Red Sea.

He is a living God.

He is a God who guides.

He is a God who raises from the dead.

He is an Eternal God.

He is a God who wants me in His Kingdom for ever.

★ ★ ★

Man's destiny is so great, his vocation so radical, that there is no room for positions of compromise or mediocrity.

'You shall love the Lord your God with all your heart, and with all your soul, and with all your might' (*Deuteronomy 6: 5*).

God truly demands everything and He Himself has told us that He is a jealous God.

But His jealousy is a different kind of jealousy from ours, and if He asks us to love Him it is because He knows that in loving Him we shall find our happiness.

It is to our interest to love Him.

In fact if we do not succeed in falling in love with God in the course of our life we are lost.

Without love we are incomplete, immature, bored, without paradise.

Indeed we could unhesitatingly establish the equation: love of God equals peace, joy, happiness, fruitfulness, exultation, paradise; not loving God equals war, unhappiness, loneliness, sterility, death, hell.

And this is why I referred to our vocation as being so radical as not to leave room for positions of mediocrity.

'You, therefore, must be perfect, as your heavenly Father is perfect' (*Matthew 5: 48*).

The requirements of the Kingdom are the very requirements of the love that by its nature finds them equal or makes them equal.

The love of God constrains us to become like God, similar to God, with the tastes of God.

There is no escape.

If God loves light then we too must love light.

If God forgives then we too must forgive.

If God dies for love then we too must be prepared to die for love.

To forge the Kingdom means no more nor less than this: to work, to act, in such a way as to become similar to God on the model of Christ.

And not in idle words, in deeds.

The Kingdom advances every time we perform a practical deed in response to the Love which is God.

When I feed the hungry
When I visit the prisoner
When I clothe the naked
When I forgive my enemy
When I share my goods
When I console the afflicted
When I pray for the living and the dead.

★   ★   ★

But the requirements of love go still further, still further than the good itself, than the works themselves, than the vocation itself.

Over and above the Promise, Abraham is the most radical example of this, and his drama is our drama, his way our way.

Listen carefully.

Hardly had Isaac – the promised son so long awaited, the purest and most precious dream of his vocation – been born to the Patriarch than he heard God say:

'Take your son . . .' (*Genesis 22*), and God told him to sacrifice his son on the mountain.

What does a request like this signify? What light emerges from the darkness of such a demand?

We know the answer well for it lies deep within each one of us, it lies in those depths where love deposits its casket of precious jewels. God's gifts are so marvellous that they tempt us to idolatry.

Isaac was becoming Abraham's idol.

Our vocation is making us proud.

The transparency of God's absoluteness is becoming dimmed within us.

'Take your son . . . and offer him' says God to the Patriarch who lives within each one of us.

God places this demand on each of His gifts.

Rather than run the risk of Isaac developing a hold on Abraham and blocking him on the path of love, or of ourselves prostrated in adoration before the good that we do, God stakes His claim.

God is greater.

The requirements of His love oblige us to go further.

We are what we have given.

And it will only be when we – Abraham and ourselves – have offered the Son of our work, offered Him sadly but unambiguously, that we shall be able to have Him again in perfect freedom.

Only the love of God as the Absolute has the power to restrain us from idolatry and keep us free.

Without our love for God each of us sooner or later becomes the slave of his vocation, the child of his child, and we block through the sterile desire for possession the never-finished path of infinite love.

★ ★ ★

When I read about Jesus's childhood in St Luke's Gospel, I never used to be able to understand how Mary and Joseph could have been so careless as to lose Jesus on that pilgrimage to Jerusalem.

I used to say to myself in my ignorance: I could never have done such a thing.

I would have attached Him to my foot with a cord, as they do with sheep in the desert, rather than have the malicious word go down in history that I, the guardian of God's son, had been so negligent as to lose Him in the big dangerous city of Jerusalem.

Now, however, I realize that losing Him was one of the most illuminating things that Mary and Joseph did, for it was a sign of their enormous freedom with regard to Jesus and, still more, with regard to the Father who is in heaven.

Mary was not a fusser; she was free enough to let her son circulate at will. Joseph on his side was not the slave of a child who nevertheless overshadowed him with the sovereignty of Mystery.

To have allowed Jesus to slip away from their surveillance illuminates to the highest degree the dignity of the faith of these two creatures.

Although the Gospel does not say it in so many words, we can see that even Joseph and Mary had accepted Abraham's sacrifice.

'Take your son . . . and offer him.'

And this was why Jesus was free, so free as to stay away from them for three days.

So free as, later, to stay three days in the bowels of the earth.

★   ★   ★

Have you understood, brother, what I've been trying to say this evening?

Do not be afraid when God calls you, but do not be afraid when He is silent.

Do not be afraid when He asks you to perform some task, but do not be afraid when He asks for it back.

Do not be afraid if He gives you a husband or a wife, but do not be afraid if He doesn't.

God is greater than His call.

God is greater than your works.

God is greater than the good that we do.

What matters is to walk towards His presence and to be certain in faith that it is He who is leading us.

YOU SHALL NOT
ESCAPE FROM LOVE

Thursday

The key to the mystery is love. God loves me like a son. It is very difficult to escape from His love. Perhaps pain tells me something about God's 'passion' for me, the passion that He tells me about in the parable of the prodigal son.

LAUDS	Psalm 22
(Morning	Psalm 38
Prayer)	Hezekiah's song (*Isaiah 38*)
VESPERS	Psalm 27
(Evening	Psalm 51
Prayer)	Job's hymn (*6, 7, 9; 16–19*)
READINGS	Isaiah 53
	Epistle to the Philippians (*the whole*)
	John 9

★　　★　　★

Last night a terrible thing happened at the fraternity.
A junkie as strong as a bull landed up with us during Mass.
Luckily the liturgy was drawing to a close and he, who couldn't

go on any longer, came out with us who couldn't go on any longer either – such was the agitation that his restless presence had bequeathed to the prayerful assembly.

In the kitchen he asked me for a coffee while fixing me with his eyes – eyes that I can hardly forget, for they looked like the eyes of an animal that had been hounded for several days and was now at the end of its strength.

His hands were trembling so violently that he spilt half his coffee on his jacket, then fell with a thud to the floor. Here he was shaken by terrible convulsions and there was vomit in his mouth.

Although there were four of us we couldn't hold him still and soon he had struck his head against a corner of the stove.

I had blood, coffee and slobber all over my hand.

Finally we got a cushion under his head where he lay on the ground because at that moment we couldn't face carrying him up to the first floor where the brothers' bunks are.

He dozed for a little while then opened his infinitely sad eyes and asked me for any kind of drug substitute.

He had endured the whole day without drugs and now just could not go on.

He started shaking again as if possessed.

Later a doctor came and gave him an injection.

Then four male nurses came and took him to hospital.

★   ★   ★

This story is the modern counterpart of St Luke's parable about the prodigal son.

In Jesus's time things were simpler and the escape from home was almost always prompted by the desire to 'devour one's living with harlots' (*Luke 15: 30*).

Men were healthier in those days.

Today they devour possessions, health and hope in the flight to drugs.

But the story is the same even if it is more dramatic and more violent.

And above all clearer.

Drugs have taught me a great deal through their ruthless logic of pleasure.

I would suggest that they have lessened the space of the isolated area where man is in flight.

Luke says that when the prodigal son had spent everything he went to a distant land.

For us there is not even the distant land. Suffice it to go round the corner and meet up with a group of like-minded people in some squalid secret room where a dose of LSD can be injected to the sound of an endless gramophone.

But I said that the isolated area is smaller round this prodigal son and the result more immediate, the consequence more radical, the lesson clearer: namely that it is impossible to live for long far from the Father: there lies death.

And this comes first.

Harlots devour more slowly and less radically than drugs.

LSD has the power of doing you much more harm.

★　　★　　★

At table in the fraternity we discussed the matter of drugs at length.

What struck us most was the junkie's herculean strength though he was in the process of being reduced to a nonentity as a result of the evil's hold on him.

The prodigal son of the parable had been in the grip of hunger;

last night's junkie was in the grip of the effects of the drug itself.

We never make much headway when following the road of our misguided tastes!

Someone or something contrives to stop us.

Never had the purpose of pain in man's life struck me so forcibly.

What would become of man without the effects of physical pain?

What would stop him?

What would warn him that he was harming himself?

What would show him the consequences of his excesses? Of the wounds he was inflicting on his nature?

Man is free to indulge in riotous living and to live by overthrowing the order of things, but on his way he will surely meet the suffering that will prostrate him.

He is free to separate himself from God who is order, nature and life, but God then surrounds him with a hedge and fills his path with thorns so that he sees that it is better to stop and perhaps even turn round and go back again.

Nature is one of God's great signs and man will never manage to elude it.

Nor will he succeed in ridding himself of the fear, indeed the terror, that death lays upon him.

In the last analysis what matters is to stop in time.

I am reminded of the story of Pinocchio. He is made of wood so is insensitive to pain.

But when he let his leg loll in the fireplace near the fire his insensitivity to pain became a great danger and threatened his life.

It seems absurd to say it, but: what would happen if there were no pain to sensitize us in time, to warn us?

What would have stopped the junkie of last night?

What would warn the alcoholic of the disorder in which he lives?

Man is so sick with sin, so thirsty for pleasure, that if there were no hedge of pain he would soon become satanic.

Nothing would interfere with his desires.

He would be perfectly prepared to trample over dead bodies if only he could satisfy his requirements.

And do we not perhaps see the same thing in the rich and the powerful: this capacity for destruction? To what lengths will a powerful man not go in his lust for possessions, in his urge to crush the weak?

Is it not perhaps better that someone or something should warn him in time, before he verifies what Matthew says in Chapter 25 of his Gospel?

'Depart from me, you cursed, into the eternal fire . . . for I was hungry and you gave me no food, I was thirsty and you gave me no drink, naked and you did not clothe me' (*Matthew 25: 41*).

★ ★ ★

Here we are. We have arrived at the precise point of the wherefore of pain. It is a warning.

As I see it. the terrible effect pain has on us, the huge fear it instils us with, is there to say: 'Now, listen. I, pain, am no more than a messenger, a sign.

'You, man, should not be afraid of me because in fact I render you a service. You should be afraid of what I represent.

'I, pain, am the sign of a temporary separation.

'I, death, am the sign of an eternal separation.

'That is what you should fear!'

★ ★ ★

67

Let us return to the parable of the prodigal son which is the best parable in the Gospel. We all play a part in it though usually we identify with the younger son.

Our flight is the proof that we do not believe in God, that we do not believe in life, light or love.

The father, who is love, knows that love cannot be imposed so He permits us to make our escape.

And off we go.

We opt for non-life rather than life, for lies rather than truth, for hate and selfishness rather than love.

And we make the experiment of flight. And what is terrifying in the parable is that if we had found what we were looking for we would never have come home again.

But by good fortune things didn't turn out as we hoped – we found acorns instead of bread, famine instead of plenty.

Even our friends were not so friendly when far from God, even our helpers didn't help that much.

Is all this to be wondered at?

Is it surprising if everything goes wrong?

I would suggest that in cases such as this things are more intelligent than we are; they try to help us by pitting themselves against us.

Woe if they did not do so, woe if they gave us a taste for what we are doing when we are destroying ourselves for ever.

*　　*　　*

And then for all we know the father plays a part of his own in poisoning our exile.

This I believe.

He has friends everywhere and more besides. For all we know he has written off to those friends living in the region where we are:

'Is my son staying with you by any chance? If so, I do beg you not to help him. It is only if you make his life difficult that he will grow to understand things.'

It is possible.

The Gospel does not say so but I think this happened.

Oh I would escape again if I could! If only there was any hope of finding a road so far from home . . .

Oh, if I could I feel I would jump over the hedge again – the one at the bottom of my master's field where he has given me these pigs to look after.

But I shall not try it again.

I know that after that hedge there will be other hedges going on indefinitely.

There will be nothing for me, except the road back again.

★   ★   ★

I once heard someone say: suffering is the proof that God doesn't exist.

It is impossible that a God who is our Father should endure the suffering of His son.

This evening I have a strong impression to the contrary.

It is precisely because He exists that He has invented suffering in order to pursue me.

Love has an inexorable logic and . . .

I know He loves me very much.

His love drives Him to poison my attempt to escape.

He does not want me to remain far away from Him, such a thought is unbearable to Him.

He has left me free to go off but has organized things in such a way that I am compelled to return.

If I loved, if I really loved, I would do the same.

69

We have to feel compassion for those who love.
Perhaps it is the only compassion that we can feel for God!

*   *   *

For those who love, separation is the ultimate evil especially if it can become eternal.
Physical pain is a trifle by comparison.
What does a little suffering matter?
What matters is to come back and to be together for ever.
Ask someone who knows about love, someone who is incapable of living after a separation from a child,
who feels utterly broken by the death of a mother,
who throws himself from a bridge after the death of a fiancée,
who is capable of waiting a lifetime for a husband to return from prison or exile.
Ask those people if you want to understand what love is, and what anguish it produces when it is disappointed, separated, shattered!
And what is our love compared with God's love?
For He it was who for love delivered His son to death so as to save us from death.

*   *   *

Yes, we always say that 'God is love' but it is difficult to understand the import of such an affirmation.
And it is precisely because we lack the terms of this problem that we do not understand the things of God.
How can we understand the word 'hell' and the word 'heaven' unless we set out from the depths of the mystery of God's love?
Let us try to bring some comparisons to our aid, but these are

only worth what they are worth and will never succeed in express-
ing the fullness contained in the mystery.

One thing is certain: when I have loved, truly loved, I have
understood that evil, true evil, consists of separation.

Separation is unbearable for someone who loves.

When I think of being separated from the person I love best,
and separated for ever, I go mad.

Try to think about this in practical terms.

The mother separated from her child
the bridegroom from the bride
friend from friend
son from father
and . . . for ever.
This is what is insupportable.

★   ★   ★

I am run over by a train and my body is cut in two.

But what is it that has been cut?

My body or my life?

A chemical combination or my light?

An agglomeration of cells or my love?

No, no-one can cut my life which is eternal.

No-one can cut my light which continues to exist.

No-one can cut my love.

We are eternal, we cannot die because we are grafted to the
eternal life which is God.

We are grafted to the light which is Christ.

We are united to the love which is the Holy Spirit.

And no-one can cut the Holy Spirit in two.

No-one can take away from us our participation in the divine
life.

But what no-one can take away from us, what no train can cut
in two, I myself can take away, I can cut it with my will.

I can sever myself from God, and this is my real death.

By severing myself from the life which is God
by severing myself from the Truth which is God
by severing myself from the Love which is God
I sever myself from God
and enter into non-life
into darkness, into hatred.

To God, who does not want such a horrendous thing to happen,
there remains the power to warn me.

And He warns me

And He warns me through pain.

★　　★　　★

It is strange that people should not see this and that they should
quarrel with pain as something irrational, something incompatible
with a God who is love.

The fact is that these people do not love and cannot understand.

If they loved they too would unsheathe their swords and so act
that the son returns home and the bride remains for ever with the
bridegroom.

No, do not fear pain, fear what it indicates.

Do not fear physical death which does not exist, fear eternal
death which physical death indicates.

Yes, fear that, as Francis would say!

And know that God has made pain and death horrible in order
to teach us that the true pain of separation is horrible and that true
death – the second – is still more horrible.

★　　★　　★

I know you've got a question to ask me, and I know what it is.

You want to know why the innocent have to suffer, why the poor have to suffer, why the Just Man had to die.

I used not to know the reason for these things.

When I discovered the reason it was Christ Himself who told me.

You ask Him this evening; He will tell you.

And perhaps He will add the phrase which meant so much to me when He was explaining that universal salvation depends on the vocation of some to pay for all.

'You shall not escape from love.'

If in the Kingdom we ask the innocent who suffered for sinners, the poor who paid for the rich, the tortured who shed blood for the powerful, whether it is just or mistaken to pay so dear, we shall hear them tell us:

'It was necessary so that no-one might escape from Love.'

THE IMPORTANCE OF
THE ACTUAL

Friday

We always find it difficult to imagine our relationship with God.
He himself advises us not to make plans. Better to accept the actual
as the means by which God begets us, touches us, makes us grow.
God is present in things, in events, in history, and it is by means of
signs that He manifests Himself.

LAUDS	Psalm 30
(Morning	Psalm 103
Prayer)	Moses' hymn (*Exodus 15*)
VESPERS	Psalm 40
(Evening	Psalm 116
Prayer)	Jonah's hymn (*Jonah 2*)
READINGS	Deuteronomy 6, 7, 8
	Ezekiel 15
	John 18, 19

★   ★   ★

A poem drawn from Chapter 8 of Genesis runs as follows:

It was hot that day
when Abraham was sitting
at the door of his tent.
He raised his eyes and looked
and saw three men
standing in front of him . . .
As soon as he saw them
he bowed to the earth and said:
O my Lord, I pray you,
do not pass by without stopping.
I shall bring you water
and I shall wash your feet
and then you will pass on . . .
And I shall bring you something to eat
and you will refresh yourselves
and then you will pass on . . .
Not by chance . . . not for nothing
did you pass by me today . . .[5]

★   ★   ★

The remark addressed by Abraham to the three men who
passed beside the oaks of Mamre one sunny afternoon has always
impressed me:

'Not by chance, not for nothing, did you pass by me today.'
This truth
is one that we could write on every event of our life,
engrave it on the first page of every historical fact,
extract it from each of our sufferings and each of our joys
'Not by chance

[5] From the song book of the Neo-catecumen Community.

75

not for nothing
did you pass
by me today . . . '
  – O pain
  – O day
  – O night
  – O death

★   ★   ★

I don't know if this has happened to you; it has to me.

I have often had difficulty in grasping the aspects of events, of things, of the actual, as making up part of a single whole of God's action upon me or on the history of man.

I have often found it easier to feel God's presence in a liturgical function than in the reading of a newspaper or the arrival of a friend.

An event, of whatever nature it may be, speaks to me less than a sunset or a night sky dotted with stars.

Especially if it is chaotic.

Or painful.

It is in this context that we can measure the smallness of our faith, the poverty of our contemplation in the streets and, what is far more serious, the extent of our alienation in religious matters.

It is not easy to live the desert in the city properly because we look on the city as being outside God's orbit, a sort of chaotic agglomeration that escapes from His power, where His will is inexorably at the mercy of men's wickedness or nature's irrationality.

Not to mention the events where pain, illness, death, are present. That's the end.

There God doesn't exist.

It would seem that God exists only in the transparency of sunrise and in the sweetness of some festivity; certainly not in an earthquake or in an illness that takes us off to hospital.

When we find ourselves thrown up against an anonymous event we have the feeling of being deceived, tricked, forgotten, wounded.

The actual becomes negative, it has no face, no significance, it does not speak to us.

We draw up all our forces against it as against an enemy or an intruder of whom we want to rid ourselves as quickly as possible.

And if this reality has somewhat larger dimensions and goes beyond our capacity to endure it, then it is a proof of God's absence.

How can God exist if babies die?

How is His presence possible if men are so evil and do me so much harm?

And are capable of declaring war!

*　　*　　*

As always it is the Gospel that helps us to understand.

Let us try to read it in the light of Abraham's remark: 'Not by chance, not for nothing, did you pass by me today.'

Was it by chance that Caesar Augustus decreed that there should be an enrolment of the Empire at the time of Quirinius?

Was it by chance that Jesus was born in Bethlehem?

Was it by chance that Nazareth was chosen for the Son's hidden life?

Was it by chance that Jesus met Peter, James and John?

Was it by chance that He led them to Mount Tabor, that He calmed the storm, that He raised Lazarus?

Was it by chance that He was arrested?

Was it by chance that He was crucified between two thieves?

And by chance that the earth shook and the sun ceased to give its light?

The birth and death of the Son of God, His insertion into the history of man, the shaping of Him through contradictions, the spitting in His face and condemning Him to death – was it all chance?

And to go on: what link is there between the Sermon on the Mount, the preaching of the Beatitudes, and Jesus's silence before Herod and His allowing himself, the Omnipotent, to be reduced to the Man of Sorrows through the iniquity of men?

Is there not a tremendous unity in the Gospel, a unity between the story of a poor man persecuted by power and the desire of God's Son to become the Innocent One, the Servant of Jahweh?

Is there no link between His death and His resurrection, and are not the facts of His life a preparation within Him for the figure of Christ?

Do you not feel the unity of the Gospel?

Take the most banal episodes, the most fortuitous encounters – do you not see them as contributing in a precise and inexorable way to the action of the story in which the life and death of God's Son is foreshadowed and fulfilled?

★ ★ ★

But where the lesson becomes even more precise is in Jesus's attitude towards the Mystery of God, towards the Father.

Jesus, like us, could certainly not have been happy about things going wrong, about truth being undermined, about the innocent suffering, about the triumph of evil, about the hungry remaining hungry, slaves remaining slaves.

And yet He, the Son of God, will pass over the face of history exactly as if He were the son of man.

Things will not change. The dead will continue to die, the innocent to be crushed, the hungry to be hungry.

If one or two of the dead are raised, if some starving person ceases to starve, this will merely be to give a sign, to anyone who believes, that messianic times have arrived, that the new Moses, Jesus, is among them; it will not mean that things are going to change, that the drudgery of work will be removed from human life, or the pain of having to die.

Anyone who wanted to see Him as a wonder-worker resolving all man's problems, a healer emptying the hospitals, was destined to disappointment.

Anyone who wanted to see Him as the leader of some brilliant political mission that would conquer everything with the introduction of miracles into the normal system of things – miracles that would in some way alter the laws of nature and the daily task – felt equally disillusioned, and abandoned Him.

The powerful abandoned Him too, those who wanted to make use of religion and the Messiah to consolidate their power.

The persecuted abandoned Him, those who did not want to be persecuted any more, and the suffering who wanted to take revenge on those who made them suffer.

Those who stayed with Him were the poor who accepted the fact of being poor, the persecuted who did not want to persecute, the mourners who understood the purpose of weeping and glimpsed through their tears the mystery of Christ and the novelty of the Beatitudes which He preached.

★   ★   ★

But Christ, the Son of God, the Omnipotent, not only did not want to change things, He did not even ask that they should be changed.

He could have asked the Father to remove death from man's life, to eliminate hunger from the earth, to overthrow tyrants, bring about justice.

He did not ask it.

As far as I know He asked one thing only: 'Father, may thy will be done' (*Matthew 6: 10*).

He saw the actual as the Father's will in action, He saw things that happen as a discourse that should be read, He saw events as signs of the times that announce the Kingdom and prepare for its coming.

Faced with real things He invited people to stop and ask the reason for them.

Faced with pain He asked them to try to understand the purpose of its presence.

And it is then that the hungry man will tell of the selfishness and greed of the rich.

The poor countries by their presence will denounce the intolerable tyranny of the rich countries, the prisons with their tortured will become the visible condemnation of those wielding power.

The dying man will remind me that the earth is not my country, and the consequences of my mistakes will show me the rightness and necessity of expiation.

Nothing can escape from the multiplicity of the actuality in which I am immersed and which helps me to be born into a new life.

★   ★   ★

What matters is to see ourselves clearly and it is not always easy to read the significance of signs and events.

Sometimes we can exchange a stone for bread and a serpent for a fish.

Luke has a parable, very short, but probing deep into the truth it puts forward:

'What father among you, if his son asks for a fish, will instead of a fish give him a serpent; or if he asks for an egg, will give him a scorpion?' (*Luke 11: 11–12*).

You must take account of the resemblance between a stone and bread, between a fish and a serpent, between an egg and a scorpion.[6]

The parable seems to be telling us: My son, I am your father and I will not give you a stone instead of bread, a serpent when you ask for fish, a scorpion if you need an egg.

It may be that a thing seems to you to be a stone, but be careful: it isn't a stone, it's bread.

It may be that an ailment appears to you as a serpent, but no, it is a fish that has nourished you and corrected you.

A misfortune may descend on you like a scorpion, but really it is an egg and it has nourished you and done you good.

'Everything contributes towards goodness for the person who believes in God,' who hopes in God, who loves God, and God will suffer 'no evil to befall you, no scourge to come near your tent' (*Psalm 91*) unless it be to transform it into grace and bring it into the plan of salvation.

Not for nothing is reading the signs of the times one of the fundamental things for the Christian and the Church!

In Pius IX's pontificate the collapse of the temporal power was not a stone to break its teeth but white bread offered to the Church by history so that she might become whiter and more desirable.

In Pius X's pontificate the modernists were not all serpents to be trodden underfoot but good fish whose constant thrashing about

---

[6] This phenomenon is to be found especially in desert places on cold nights. The scorpion curls up and covers itself with a white downy shell which to a passer-by can look very like an egg.

in stagnant waters forced the Church to come out of her immo-
bilism and prepare herself for the Council to come.

In Pius XII's pontificate socialism and the political defeats of so-
called Christians were not scorpions to be afraid of; no, they were
eggs whose nourishment could have contributed to an understanding that situations of power can become anti-evangelical, and
that for the Christian the most appropriate position to find himself
in is the opposition, like the Baptist shouting his: 'It is not lawful'
(*Matthew 14: 4*).

But how difficult it is to see ourselves properly in the signs of
the times, and how clever we Christians are at seeing blessedness
in power and riches, and in changing the blessedness of poverty
and persecution into something to be cursed and trodden underfoot.

★　　★　　★

But the Gospel condemns us.

It condemns me when I try to save myself with the device of idle
chat which is far from God's will; it condemns the Church when
she moves away from poverty and camouflages her desire to live
comfortably with the excuse of dignity or the prudence of
diplomacy.

Never has a generation been so able to understand whether I am
making accommodations or whether I am living the Gospel.

It is a generation that responds with indifference and absenteeism
to pious and devout accommodation, but to the lived Gospel it
responds with enthusiasm.

Because it is deeds that count, not empty worn-out words.

Deeds that become signs, that become prophecy.

I would like to be Pope for just one day! I may be mistaken, but
what joy I would feel if I sold the whole Vatican to the highest
bidder and went to live in a little apartment on the outskirts of

the city, or, better still, in a tent between the desert and the steppe.

Utopia?

Of course, but a utopia that does good like all the utopias of the Gospel.

And the young would be so ready for utopia!

Especially today.

★   ★   ★

It may be that the idea of selling the Vatican and its museums so as to transform the resulting space into leper villages has filled you with enthusiasm, as it has me.

But do you want to understand the illogicality of our enthusiasm, or rather the injustice of it?

This evening, when I was thinking not about other people's things but my own, I noticed that my little room was warmer than the room of the brothers with whom I live, the bed softer, my life in general more comfortable.

For one reason or another I am always at the top of the queue and I always leave the last place to the weakest and most silent.

This means that if I were Pope, even for just one day, I wouldn't do a single thing to implement my ideas.

In the Church it is all too easy to ask others to make great prophetic gestures, to embrace poverty, to share possessions.

The difficult thing is to ask it of ourselves, to live it ourselves.

I recall a Latin American writer, one famous for his fine writing and protests about torture and social injustice, and the necessity of revolution.

He himself told me that when it came to the crunch, when he was in danger of being arrested after a military coup, he fled from his country on the first aeroplane, carrying with him the shame of his cowardice, because he knew full well that he had left behind him the poorest and least protected.

Brothers, it is difficult to bear witness.

And it is precisely when we feel incapable of doing this that we risk hiding ourselves behind fine words!

Listen to the intentions formulated during the prayer of the faithful in the various church groups we belong to. You would think we were all heroes, all determined to divest the Church of her riches.

Then let us look at ourselves to see whether our actions correspond to our words.

Where have we got to in the matter of sharing our possessions?

And is it for this reason that, not wanting to be rhetorical, I ought to say this evening, not 'If I were Pope', but 'If I were Brother Carlo, what would I now do to make the Gospel actual in my life?'

What ought I to do in practical terms if I want to respond to Jesus when He says to me, as He said to Zacchaeus, 'Make haste and come down; for I must stay at your house today'? (*Luke 19: 5*).

MARANATHA

Saturday

Come, Lord Jesus, prayed the early Christians of the communities of Ephesus. This always remains the prayer of difficult times, of times like our own in which faith is purified in darkness and God reveals Himself in the transparency of lived Love.

LAUDS   Psalm 62
(Morning   Psalm 124
  Prayer)   Ezekiel's song (*36*)

VESPERS   Psalm 69
(Evening   Psalm 91
  Prayer)   Mary's hymn (*Luke 1*)

READINGS   Jeremiah 20
            John 14
            Matthew 25

★   ★   ★

I call to mind the big cities that I have visited in the course of my life: New York, Bangkok, São Paulo, Rio de Janeiro, Chicago, Hong Kong, Buenos Aires, London, Oslo, Paris, Madrid, Dakar,

Fez, Algiers, Cairo, Baghdad, Teheran, Calcutta and all the other innumerable centres of habitation, including small villages, where I have been for reasons of the Gospel.

In all my travels it is true to say that I have never been attracted anywhere for touristic reasons: I have been spurred on my way purely by eagerness for the apostolate and the Mystery of the Church.

In every city I have prayed with my brothers in the faith, with those who, like me, are trying to live the Gospel in the footsteps of Christ.

This has been one of God's great gifts to me, for with its help I have navigated the boat of my life along a river swollen with friendships, and my hope has been nourished in the warmth of liturgical gatherings.

What endless conversations, day after day, night after night, on the favourite theme of God and the Church!

When I think of my brothers scattered all over the world I understand what is meant by spiritual fatherhood, and I often experience the pain of distance.

How I would love to be near all of them this evening.

To be able to say: courage!

Yes, courage in tribulation

courage in temptation

courage in faith.

I know what you are going through, overworked as you are, surrounded by the pressures of the crowd, worried by responsibilities of all kinds, anxious for peace and prayer.

To many of you I would not hesitate to apply St Paul's words to the Corinthians:

> We are afflicted in every way, but not crushed; perplexed, but not driven to despair; persecuted, but not forsaken; struck

down, but not destroyed; always carrying in the body the death of Jesus (*2 Corinthians 4: 8*).

Because we are living in hard times and it is not easy to keep the faith.

Dear comrades in the faith!

I imagine you returned from work, either by train or hurrying on foot through the crowds. I imagine you sitting at your table in your room and resting from the labours of the day. I imagine the city lights being switched on in the dark outside.

It does me good to think of myself united with you all – the ideal family as the Bible calls 'the people of God' – a family which shares the same faith and is called to the same hope wherever its members are scattered throughout the world.

You are witnesses to the Invisible, believers in the one God, worshippers of the Spirit, partisans of the Kingdom of Heaven, waiting in the desert of the city for the return of Christ, whispering like the early Christians: Maranatha – Come, Lord Jesus!

★　　★　　★

Yes, Christians watch and pray. Their house is like a convent, the ideal of a modern convent.

They wage a brave battle against the danger denounced by Luke concerning the last days:

When the Son of Man comes, will he find faith on earth (*Luke 18: 8*).

It isn't a joke as they know full well.

They are fighting the toughest battle of their lives.

The chaos of the city poses a continual challenge to the littleness of their faith: 'Where is your God?' (*Psalm 42: 3*).

Disorder, violence, the collapse of ancient traditions bang at the door and shout in their ears: 'Where is your God?'

> Why are you cast down, O my soul,
> and why are you disquieted within me?
> Hope in God; for I shall again praise Him,
> my help and my God (*Psalm 42: 5*).

★   ★   ★

Faith today is difficult. This is an indisputable sign of our times.

The collapse of cultures has stripped it bare, the death of civilization has filled it with sorrow. I would say that today we discover God more easily in His negative. Normally we do not hear His melody when He whispers, but when He is silent, then we build.

Another reason why man feels alone is because the Churches have been taken by surprise and gripped by panic and they often think that the way to save themselves is by looking to the past instead of marching towards the newness of God with the trust of children.

We are living in apocalyptic times and seldom before has John's book provided such a good text for prayer.

Says the Lord:

> I am the Alpha and the Omega,
> the Beginning and the End.
> To the thirsty I will give
> water without price
> from the fountain of Life (*Apocalypse 21: 6*).

And for the person who is frightened of loneliness:

Behold, the dwelling of God is with men.
He will dwell with them,
and they shall be his people,
and God himself shall be with them (*Apocalypse 21: 3*).

And for the person who suffers and is afraid:

He will wipe away every tear
from their eyes,
and death shall be no more,
neither shall there be mourning nor crying nor pain any more,
for the former things have passed away . . .
Behold, I make all things new (*Apocalypse 21: 4–5*).

But where the Apocalypse can really provide the most illuminating text for the days in which we live is in its attitude of waiting
for God who is coming, for Christ who is returning.

Maranatha! prayed St John's community at Ephesus. Come,
Lord Jesus! (*Apocalypse 22: 20*)

The Christians of our immediate past were able to have some
quiet corner where they could rest their eyes and be fed by optimism: a Church organized and triumphant, a respectable number of
believers, a civilization that at least appeared to be Christian,
decent pious families.

But today!

No, with the weakening of belief in the Church-in-terms-of-
numbers and its substitution by belief in the Church-in-terms-
of-signs, things have very much changed. Some people do not
understand any more and they suffer.

Anyone who looks at the reality of today without a prophetic
spirit finds that optimism is dead.

But surely you all know that when human optimism dies
Christian hope is born?

Optimism means faith in men, in the human potential; hope means faith in God and in His omnipotence.

So we live in apocalyptic times, that is to say times when the believer looks at heaven before he looks at the earth, when he seeks the signs of God's coming rather than the ferment of the nations, when he looks to God's fidelity rather than to men's ability or cunning.

And even when he acts his spirit is steeped in faith in the word

Maranatha!
Come, Lord Jesus!

★   ★   ★

And this evening I, too, want to come to you, brother or sister. Do you know why?

To bear witness to you in the Holy Spirit that God is the Living God.

Because this is the task of the Christian community: to bear witness to our belief to each other.

And I bear witness to it before you: I believe!

You do not see God in things
and He is in things.

You do not see God in history
and He is in history.

You do not see God in your room
and He is in your room
He is there where you are at this minute.

And He is looking at you and wants to communicate with you from the depths of His being.

And it is your faith that makes Him present to you.

God, the true God, is the God of our faith: there is no other God but Him.

It is with Him that we have a relationship; it is Him we discover in the deepness of things.

Sometimes we almost have the impression that He is a God invented by ourselves, created by our thirst for Him, so great is our freedom and so important is our duty to believe, but rest assured of this: He is the one and only God who reveals Himself to man.

The only road He treads so as to come to us and reveal Himself to us is that same road that we tread in order to seek Him. We find Him in the measure in which we believe, no more, no less.

And, you must believe it, there is nothing to be done to alter things.

How many times have I thought: if only there could be other ways, easier ways, more visible, more credible.

I have never found them.

They do not exist.

God has laid it down that the colloquy with Him takes place in faith, that growth in Him is forged in hope, and that the revelation of Him is tested in charity.

And this until the very end, that is to say until the last day, the day when 'we shall rise from the dead'.

★　　★　　★

But let us try to imagine some other system, some method of encounter between God and ourselves that is different, that does not depend on faith.

This, for instance: an encounter where His visibility makes itself present to me as an unexpected light, as a human presence, as a perceptible voice, or something else of the kind.

What good would it do?

Apart from the danger of a heart attack, who could tell me for sure that a presence of this kind was the presence of God and not of a ghost?

No–one.

So we are brought back to faith even in a case such as this; we have to call faith into service.

It was through faith that Abraham believed the voice that said to him, Leave your country; it was through faith that Moses read God's presence in the burning bush; it was through faith that Joseph agreed to look on his dream as God's will and to take Mary for his betrothed.

God's word clothes faith with images, voices, angels, thunder, that is to say with an idiom suited to our weakness, but the real problem remains: as long as we are on earth the encounter between Him and ourselves remains an encounter of faith.

Try to imagine that God's presence manifests itself in you, near you, as simple people normally think, as a person, as yourself, and that this human presence stands there with a dense and reasonable visibility, outside the Mystery; then how would you be able to move?

How could you feel at your ease?

How could a presence such as this help you?

It would constitute such a conditioning that you would be unable to move.

It would put a limit to the space of your freedom, and you would find yourself confronted, as it were, with a superior watching over you, an inspector scrutinizing you.

Your gestures would become conditioned, your reactions clumsy and inaccurate as when you are frightened.

I want you to be convinced: dark faith is the space of your freedom.

It is in this space that we must grow up, and grow up into gratuitous love.

Pascal would say, 'to act as if . . .'.

Yes, as if He were there and you saw Him.

But by not seeing Him with the eyes of the flesh, you are free.

The things that you do are worth what they are worth, without deceits, without conditionings.

Yes, only in faith are you truly free, and your actions count in His eyes because they are dictated by love alone and not by fear of His presence.

Remember we are not yet grown up as sons, we are still slaves of His power and His greatness.

★   ★   ★

Act as if . . .

I shall act as if . . .

I do act as if . . .

To act as if God were present!

But this is yet another journey.

You will achieve maturity when you no longer put the question which, in the last analysis, is only a little assistance for immature children.

It is not necessary to do things as if God were present and watching you.

You should do things because they must be done, because your 'yes' which you have brought to maturity is the same as God's 'yes', because the truth with which those things are clothed is the same as God's truth, and the love that requires you to do them is the same as God's love.

You should do them as God would do them.

And by doing them as He would do them you enter into the full maturity of His son.

Christ on the cross did this, and by His sorrowful 'My God, my

God, why hast thou forsaken me?' (*Matthew 27, 45*) He bears witness to the true freedom with which God invested men, to the infinite trust which the Father puts in them, to the total lack of manipulation in the maturing of the extreme gift of themselves to the Absolute. And they offer themselves to His absent Presence.

What an extraordinary value does man's action acquire!

What dignity invests this radical attitude!

Yes, we can say it: if God is great in His essence, man is great when he draws near to Him, when as a free choice he does the things that God does.

What value does martyrdom acquire, and indeed action of any kind, when achieved in this solitude!

God's absence allows man to offer himself totally in the freedom of love as he treads the way of the cross.

If the dark night were sweetened by any sensible presence, then martyrdom would no longer be martyrdom and man's weaknesses would become servility or fear.

Have you understood, brother, why God is dead in your dark faith?

Why He does not make Himself felt at your request, exactly as if He were dead?

It is so as to allow you to die of love too, just as Jesus did in His terrible solitude.

That is how it is, and that is how it has to be.

If you sought God's sensible presence, His presence in fantasy, in reasoning, you would only have a tiny bit of help from it, help which would let you down at the first puff of wind.

By seeking instead His presence in faith, you will be sustained in your belief; by longing to touch God in hope, you will feel impelled into the depths of His light; by living His charity you will know God in the contemplation that He Himself will give you.

You will know the vertiginousness of God.
You will see the heavens open.

★   ★   ★

Now I would like to tell you something very important about the way to make God's presence visible in our life.

A pity I discovered it too late!

I have behaved like the man who travels over mountains and seas to look for a treasure, then returns home exhausted and discovers to His surprise that the treasure is in his house.

There you are: God is in your house.

In my house, in your house, in Mother Teresa's house in Calcutta, in Martin Luther King's house, in Roger Schutz's house, in Follerau's house.

As He is a hidden God no-one sees Him, but everyone seeks Him because everyone longs to see Him.

The whole business is extraordinarily interesting!

But while I'm thinking about the best way of discovering God, of seeing God, and while you're studying the problem, Mother Teresa goes out into the streets and sees someone dying alone and without help. She does not rationalize about God, or work out a five-year plan, or theorize about mankind.

She comforts the dying man, she gets help to carry him into the house, she gives him water to drink, she combs his hair, she wipes away his deathly sweat, she thinks to herself with tenderness: 'I want him to die knowing a friend is near.' Not at all an ambitious programme, not a revolution, just a true act of love.

Brothers, confronted with Mother Teresa the world stands still for a moment: it sees God passing down the streets of Calcutta.

And what did Martin Luther King do? He looked around him and loved passionately his despised brothers, his brothers despised for the colour of their skin, and he offered his breast to a discharge of bullets. The world was aware that God was there in the action of this martyr.

And what did Roger Schutz do? He, too, looked around him; he looked outside his convent walls and saw many young people wishing to believe, to hope, to communicate.

He loved them and they understood and we saw the epic of Taizé. God revealed himself at Taizé.

And you can carry on.

God reveals himself where there is anyone who respects life, who desires the light, who seeks to love. Every time you open yourself to life, every time you act the truth, every time you love, God is there in your action.

It is as if you were creating your God.

And this is why I said that God is within things

within events

within your gestures of love.

By doing things as Jesus would do them, as God would do them, you free God from the veils of invisibility and make Him visible on man's journey.

Faith is an act, not a series of idle remarks.

Hope is an undertaking bathed in light, not a pious sentiment.

Charity is an event, not a devotional little prayer.

JESUS'
PROPHECY

Sunday

The true prophecy of Jesus is as follows: You are risen in Jesus
Christ. Thus seek for the things of heaven. The resurrection is the
victory of God in man and the transmission to him of power over
impossible things, such as living the Beatitudes. Especially the
Beatitude of poverty and chastity.

LAUDS	Psalm 114
(Morning	Psalm 148
Prayer)	The song of the three young men (*Daniel 3*)
VESPERS	Psalm 2
(Evening	Psalm 110
Prayer)	Epistle to the Colossians (*1*)
READINGS	Jonah (*all*)
	Apocalypse 21, 22
	Luke 24

★　　★　　★

On my last visit to Bangkok, my brother – who is not only a
bishop, but the Christian representative in ecumenical encounters

with Buddhists and Muslims who constitute by far the biggest religious groups in Thailand – my brother told me that one of the results obtained from these encounters was a plan to build a place of prayer, an ashram (to use the Hindu word) which would be common to all religions.

The site had already been chosen, it was a pleasant lonely valley topped by three small hills.

On these three hills three monuments would be built, one to Buddha, one to Muhammad and one to Jesus, and these would dominate the huts of those at prayer and those seeking union with God in contemplation.

I was delighted by the idea for I am one of those who believe that prayer unites whereas culture often divides, and I made up my mind yet again to take part in some encounter in prayer with Buddhist and Muslim brothers.

My brother asked me what I thought should be inscribed beneath the monument to Jesus.

I had no hesitation in telling him that I would write:

'This is Jesus who, by rising from the dead, announced to men their own resurrection.'

★   ★   ★

It is not difficult to come to the conviction that Christ's true prophecy is the Resurrection of the dead.

I think this is really the essence of His teaching, of His 'news', rendered authentic and terribly true by the fact that He Himself rose first, thereby opening the way for ever, a way that had been awaited for centuries with the agony of each and every death.

It is enough to see an animal dying with its flesh lacerated, enough to see a man in his last agony, to understand that an unbearable question mark hangs over nature in all its guises, a tragedy without end, unremitting darkness.

No-one has been able to offer an answer. Words become irrelevant when a cry of distress comes from a living body, and the most we can do is to say with Job:

> Let the day perish wherein I was born,
> and the night which said,
> 'A man-child is conceived' (*Job 3: 2*).

Creation was very patient to endure death for so many generations until finally He came to explain things.

Certainly creation was helped by the Holy Spirit who dwelt within it to give it the strength to wait, otherwise it would not have been capable of waiting.

The capacity to die gives honour to flowers, to birds, to foxes, to men.

I am always moved when I see an ant that I have carelessly crushed, or a rabbit looking at me with vacant eyes while I slit its throat open with a knife to prepare dinner for my brothers.

Woe if I try to understand!

Better to live in the pages of a fairy story where life and death meet each other as if this were the most natural thing and there were nothing frightening about it.

★   ★   ★

And John does not frighten us either when he shows us death in the image of a grain of wheat that dies.

'Truly, truly, I say to you, unless a grain of wheat falls into the earth and dies, it remains alone; but if it dies, it bears much fruit' (*John 12: 24*).

It is such a vital image that it has the power to distract us from the picture of the little grain decomposing into death. Our attention is immediately drawn to the marvel of what happens afterwards: thirty or forty seeds have shot up into the sunlight, all fruit of the one dead one that we don't think about any more.

This is exactly what happens to the woman – and the comparison is again from John – who 'when in travail has sorrow . . . but when she is delivered of the child, she no longer remembers the anguish, for joy that a child is born into the world' (*John 16: 21*).

The Gospel is preparing us for the great explanation of the wherefore of pain and death, it is showing us the mystery hidden in the centuries, 'life is born from death'.

When we have seen the whole of life breaking through, we shall forget the fear we felt on the road to death.

It is no good concealing it. The Gospel is eschatological.

In the intermediate stages it leaves you with your heart in suspense.

This is why only children know how to trust, or can live without dying of fear.

Yes, life is born from death, the resurrection breaks through from total destruction.

But if we look deep inside ourselves we discover something very important, something fundamental.

The resurrection is not the exhumation of a corpse.

It is something quite different . . . keep calm.

Imagine, for example, that with the help of care and pills your body has reached the age of 95, and in its weakness and ugliness cries out to disappear; imagine it seeing itself re-appearing just like that after the resurrection.

What a calamity!

If God's power in the resurrection were that of exhuming a corpse, I would say to Him humbly but earnestly that, as far as I was concerned, 'Lord, please leave me in the earth and don't let anyone see my face again'.

If you really want to make use of the compost of my body then let a flower grow over it.

And that's enough.

No, brothers and sisters (to whom beauty is even more important), no, the resurrection is not the exhumation of a corpse, however beautiful this may be, if, for instance, it were the body of a beautiful girl who has had the good fortune to die at twenty, or that of Pascoli's young friend whom the poet thus remembered on his death bed:

> It were better to die while your head was fair
> So that when on the pillow it lay
> Your mother combed into waves that lovely hair
> But gently, not to hurt you or dismay.

There is someone else who combs our hair when it is reduced to stringy wisps by life's suffering and bathed in deathly sweat.

It is the God of Life who draws near to our death, our death rendered more deathlike by sin, by the experience of suffering, and He breathes as He did that first time at the genesis of the universe, and He says:

'I make all things new', so I make you new too.

I make you as you desired to be.

Did you want to love but never managed to: now you will.

Did you want chastity and did you weep for your failures? Look at yourself now, I make you chaste.

Did you dream of saving everyone, and did you wake up every morning humiliated by your selfishness and your fears? Look, I make you able to communicate with all the poor of the universe, and to live the gift of yourself.

★　★　★

The resurrection is not the exhumation of my corpse. That has ceased to exist like the grain of wheat that fell into the earth.

It is nothing more than the sign of something else that is dawning: the memory of a true story, my story, a continuity in which the best of me, my consciousness, has found its milieu, and has developed its divine reality as a son of God.

The resurrection is God's triumph within us, the proof of His creative power, His capacity to make all things new.

It's amazing!

Isaiah had prophesied it:

> For behold, I create new heavens and a new earth;
> and the former things shall not be remembered
> or come into mind.
> But be glad and rejoice for ever
> in that which I create (*Isaiah 65: 17*).

And John, his eyes bewitched by love, says:

> And I saw the holy city, new Jerusalem,
> coming down out of heaven from God,
> prepared as a bride
> adorned for her husband (*Apocalypse 21: 2*).

This is my body risen from the dead, the new Jerusalem which goes to meet its God, the new heavens of Isaiah, my Land which has become God's possession.

★   ★   ★

And it goes to meet Him now.

This land of mine which has become God's possession acquires the capacity contained in Christ's resurrection. And we can formulate the reason for this. We do not say, 'We shall rise', we say, 'We have risen'.

Just as the Incarnation brings the 'I' of God to birth in the Land of Mary which is our Land, so the resurrection brings the transforming and salvific power of Jesus's resurrection to all the visible reality of the cosmos and history.

It is the whole of reality that becomes capable of rising, of being made new, of being deified.

Jesus's resurrection makes it impossible for man's story to end in chaos – it has to move inexorably towards light, towards life, towards love.

And we the redeemed, who have the first fruits of the Spirit, are the first to bear witness to it.

And this is why the Kingdom is already among us.

And this is why the Gospel is not only an eschatological message but also a message of 'today'.

As we are already risen we have the power of the things up above, the capacity to live the impossible things of the Spirit: the Beatitudes.

It is enough to desire to.

The power of Jesus's resurrection, God's capacity to 'make all things new', is transmitted to our nature as men.

Henceforward it is not madness to say

> Blessed are the poor in spirit
> Blessed are those that mourn
> Blessed are the meek
> Blessed are those who hunger and thirst for righteousness
> Blessed are the merciful
> Blessed are the pure in heart
> Blessed are the peacemakers
> Blessed are those who are persecuted for righteousness' sake
> (*Matthew 5: 3–10*).

★　　★　　★

But let us make it plain: the capacity to live the Beatitudes is due to Christ's resurrection. And it is because we are already 'risen in Him' that we can do it.

To call suffering, mourning, poverty and persecution 'blessed' is not normal procedure for man-Adam.

Only man-Jesus was able to think it and live it and later communicate it as His secret.

But you understand that a secret like this – the joy of being poor, the joy of being persecuted, the joy of being chaste – is on such a high level and surrounded by such delicacy that it can only be lived in and through a very exceptional love.

And, still more, in absolute freedom.

It cannot be imposed.

Just as all the absolutes cannot be imposed but have to be accepted freely in love.

Even God does not impose it, He proposes it.

And we must do the same.

How is it possible for Christians who understand the value of freedom to impose on others the absolutes of poverty or chastity?

I can feel enthusiastic about an ordered society like a convent, a society where everyone dresses in the same way, eats more or less the same quantity of rice, and where everyone shares their goods, as I seemed to see in China.

But if I become aware that the order is imposed – as of course it is – I cannot accept it because it destroys my essence as a free man.

I can feel enthusiastic about a Church where every man has one wife and only one, where there is no divorce and everything happens in an orderly way. But as soon as I become aware that this is imposed by civil law then I rebel because I feel my freedom is destroyed.

Not even God has imposed celibacy on man and the chastity of having only one wife (his friend Abraham had two, and his forebear David had . . . ! !).

The absolute of chastity is something so lofty and so closely linked to love as to halt even God on the threshold of man's 'yes'.

How crude are certain discourses concerning the unity of marriage based on the law and delivered by Christians who remember all about Jesus apart from the Beatitudes.

And that's quite a lot!

★   ★   ★

Which doesn't mean that it is impossible to discourse on chastity and marital union and the respect for life.

Indeed I can do this and I must. But in a suitable setting.

And if I appeal to civil law I do so as a citizen who respects the multiplicity of cultures and the authentic difficulties of man's story as living a life not yet permeated by the Gospel.

And above all, in order to leave everyone free, I vote for minorities and try not to impose my religious ideas through the strength of numbers.

But if I appeal to divine law, the law which Jesus has implanted in my heart and for loyalty to which I am prepared to die, then I change my tone and say:

Brothers and sisters!

God in His son Jesus has freed us from the dark powers of paganism, of permissiveness, of money, of Eastern and Western materialism, and has arranged for us to live in His Kingdom of light and love.

We are not like those who do not believe in Christ's resurrection and who live as if invisible things did not exist.

Through God's mercy we believe in Jesus risen from the dead, and from Him we draw the strength to live on this earth as He has taught us in the Gospel.

105

Others may divorce, but not us.

Other women may have abortions through weakness or ignorance or poverty, but not our women because we believe in life.

For us love isn't the embrace of a body but a total gift of ourselves to a creature whom we love as God loves us and whom we cannot deceive at any moment.

This way of loving binds us to chaste living which is not easy, indeed it would be impossible if we were not already 'risen in Christ' and if we did not obtain help through our prayer.

We do not impose chastity on others but we want to live it ourselves as testimony that we believe in the invisible God who lives in each one of us and who calls us to freedom and salvation.

To be chaste means to respect our own body and the body of others.

To be chaste means to look at others with the eyes of a child, believing that true love is possible, that on this earth the marvel will never vanish of a boy and girl capable of giving themselves totally, radically, for ever, as if their love were already a piece of heaven.

To be chaste means to have control over oneself so that it cannot happen that our child is the fruit of casual fornication but of loving and conscientious fatherhood and motherhood, accepted as a free choice and with a joy embedded in the very mystery of God.

To be chaste means to see things with the pure eye of Jesus who, in his messianic vision, wanted the whole universe to be drawn into the dazzling potency of the resurrection in which man's very sin would be conquered, destroyed and forgotten.

And, finally, to be chaste means to have in our hearts the dream of Mary, mother of Christ and our mother, who in her infinite smallness and humility was able to live the requirements of virginity and motherhood at the same time and in the same body.